Horse Riding Schooling Progress Journal

Equine Addicts

Copyright 2020

This Book belongs to

Name _____

Address _____

_____

_____

My top goals to achieve in 20_ _

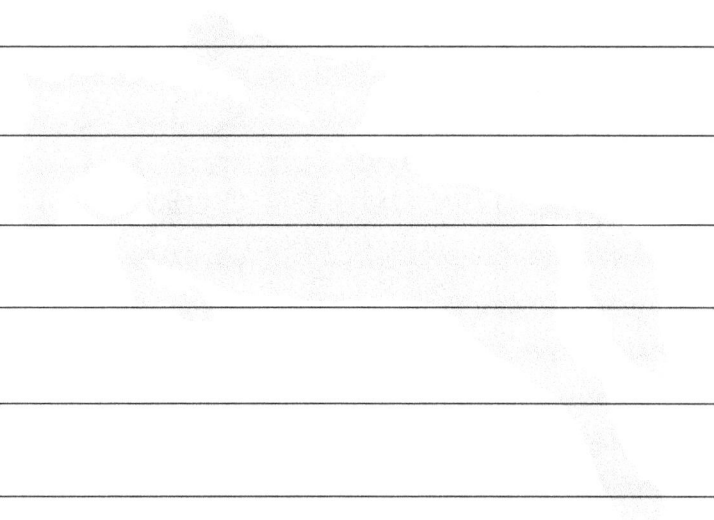

_____

_____

_____

_____

_____

_____

Date _____ Time _____

Horse _____

Instructor _____

Discipline _____

The Lessons objectives

_____

_____

_____

Instructors comments

_____

_____

_____

Positive outcome of lesson

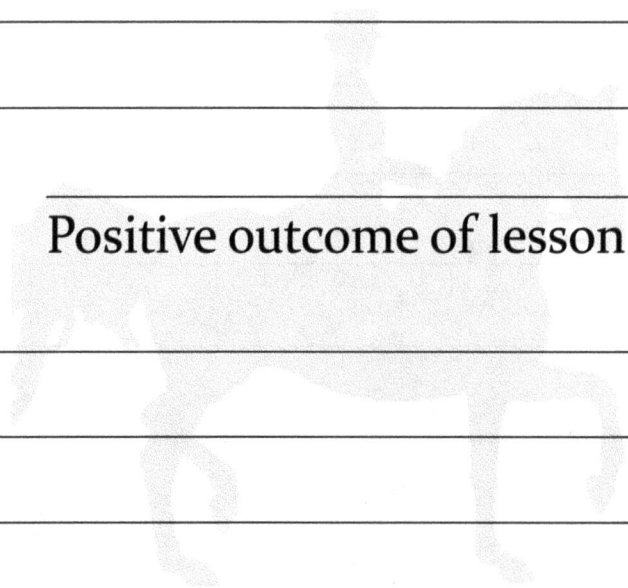

_____

_____

_____

About my performance

_____

_____

_____

_____

About my Horses performance

_____

_____

_____

_____

Transitions to practise

_____

_____

_____

_____

Exercises to practise

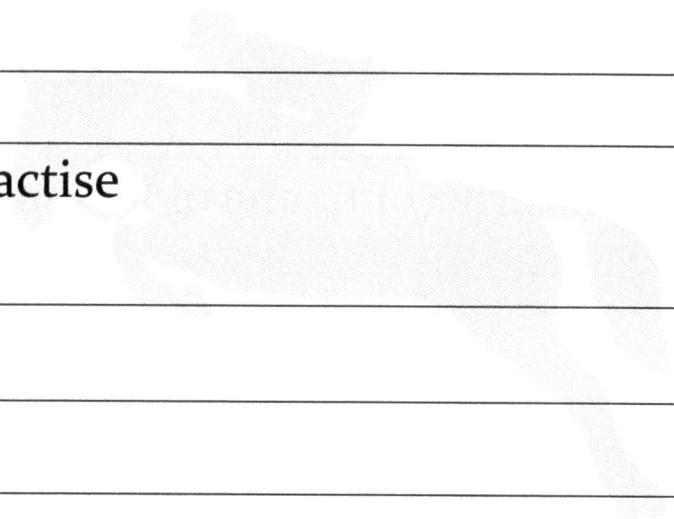

_____

_____

_____

Date _____   Time _____

Horse   _____

Instructor   _____

Discipline   _____

The Lessons objectives

_____

_____

_____

Instructors comments

_____

_____

_____

Positive outcome of lesson

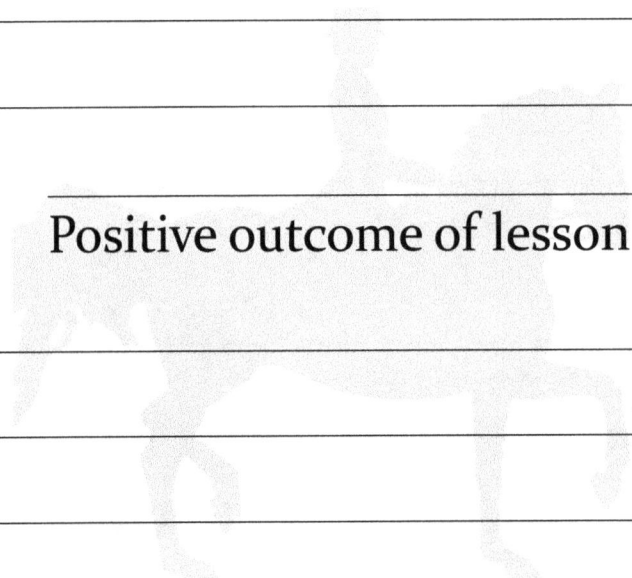

_____

_____

_____

About my performance

_____

_____

_____

About my Horses performance

_____

_____

_____

Transitions to practise

_____

_____

_____

Exercises to practise

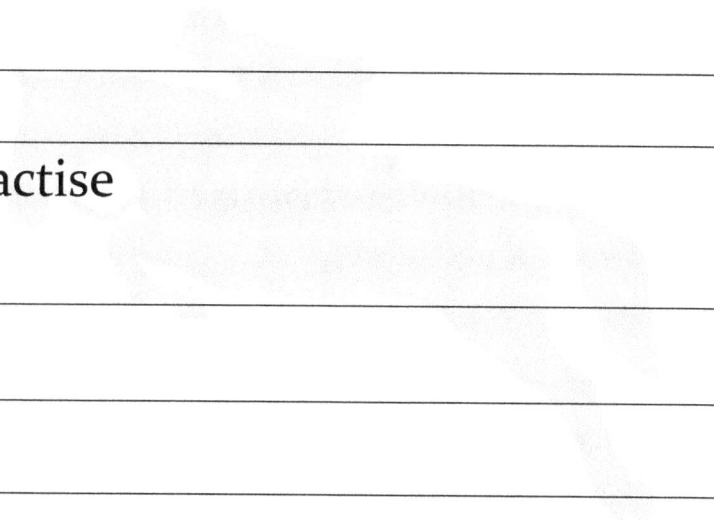

_____

_____

_____

Date _____   Time _____

Horse _____

Instructor _____

Discipline _____

The Lessons objectives

_____

_____

_____

Instructors comments

_____

_____

_____

Positive outcome of lesson

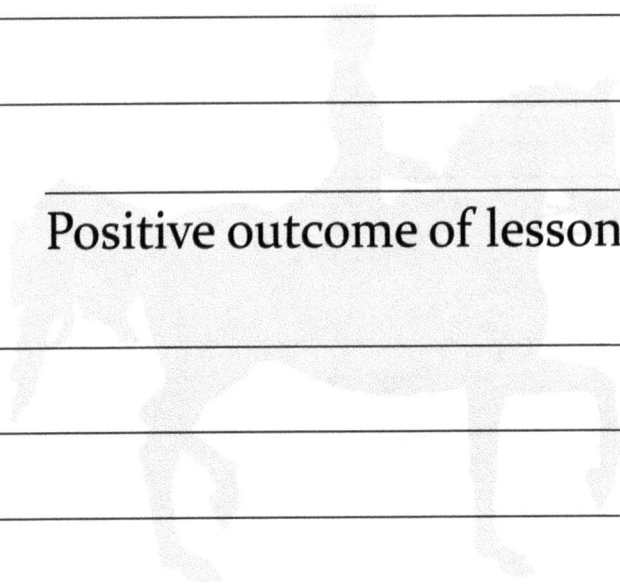

_____

_____

_____

About my performance

_____

_____

_____

About my Horses performance

_____

_____

_____

Transitions to practise

_____

_____

_____

Exercises to practise

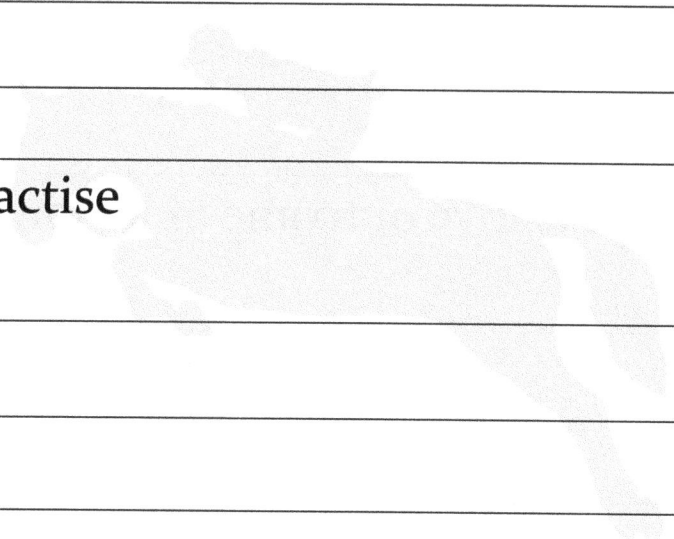

_____

_____

_____

Date ——————   Time ——————

Horse ————————————————————

Instructor ————————————————————

Discipline ————————————————————

The Lessons objectives

————————————————————————

————————————————————————

————————————————————————

Instructors comments

————————————————————————

————————————————————————

————————————————————————

Positive outcome of lesson

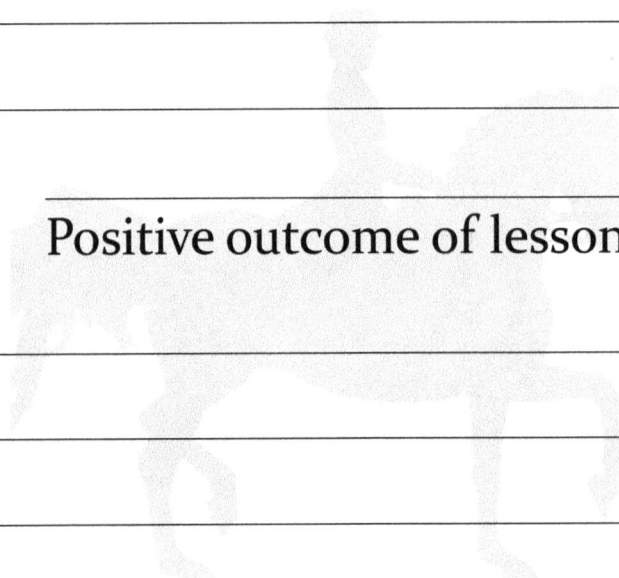

————————————————————————

————————————————————————

————————————————————————

About my performance

_____

_____

_____

About my Horses performance

_____

_____

_____

Transitions to practise

_____

_____

_____

Exercises to practise

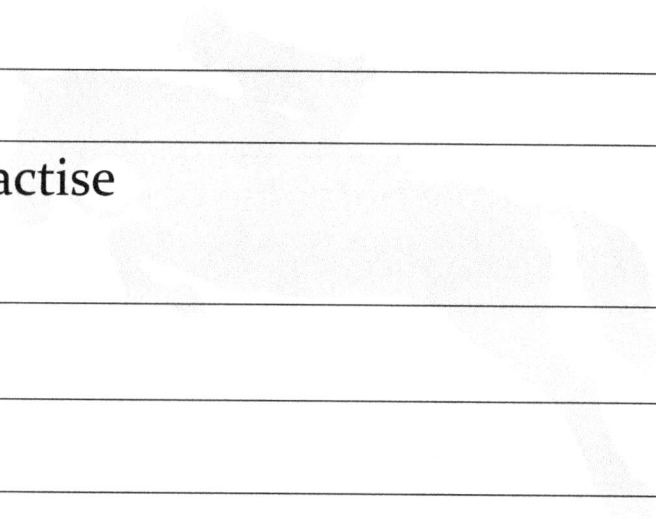

_____

_____

_____

Date _____   Time _____

Horse _____

Instructor _____

Discipline _____

The Lessons objectives

_____

_____

_____

Instructors comments

_____

_____

_____

Positive outcome of lesson

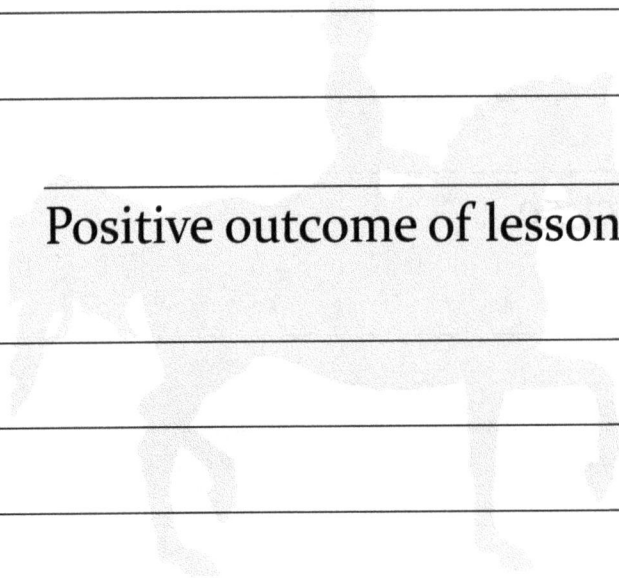

_____

_____

_____

About my performance

_____

_____

_____

About my Horses performance

_____

_____

_____

Transitions to practise

_____

_____

_____

Exercises to practise

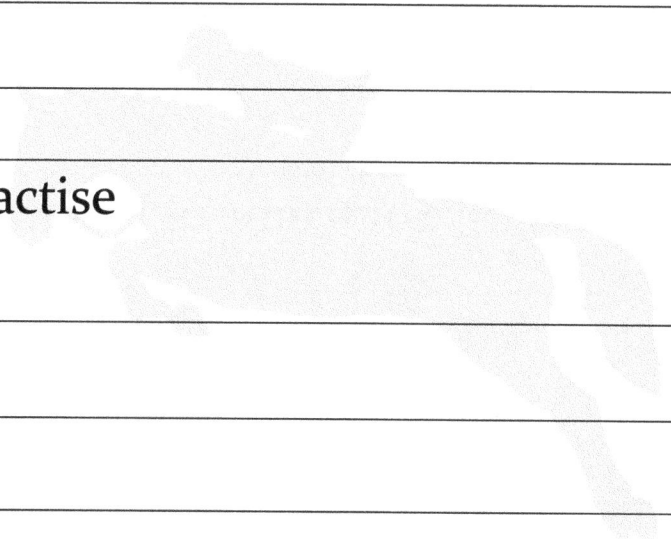

_____

_____

_____

Date _____   Time _____

Horse _____

Instructor _____

Discipline _____

The Lessons objectives

_____

_____

_____

Instructors comments

_____

_____

_____

Positive outcome of lesson

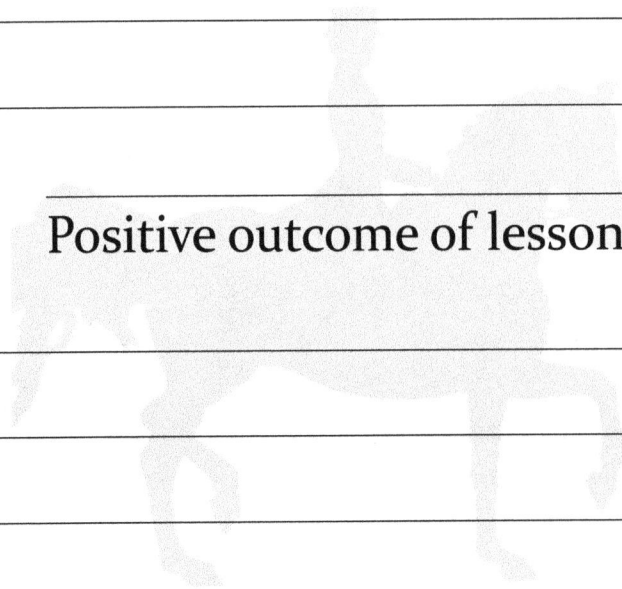

_____

_____

_____

About my performance

_____

_____

_____

About my Horses performance

_____

_____

_____

Transitions to practise

_____

_____

_____

Exercises to practise

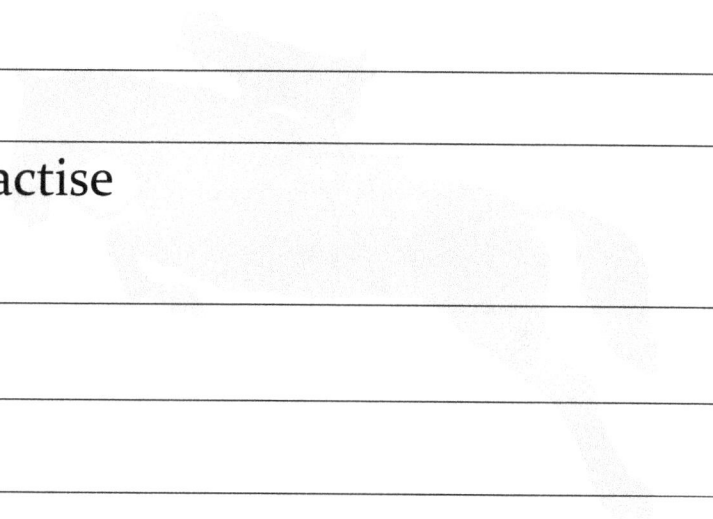

_____

_____

_____

Date _____   Time _____

Horse _____

Instructor _____

Discipline _____

The Lessons objectives

_____

_____

_____

Instructors comments

_____

_____

_____

Positive outcome of lesson

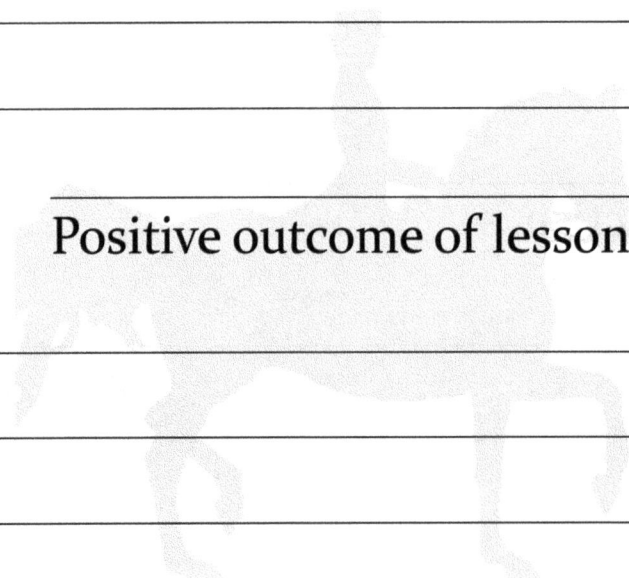

_____

_____

_____

About my performance

_____

_____

_____

About my Horses performance

_____

_____

_____

Transitions to practise

_____

_____

_____

Exercises to practise

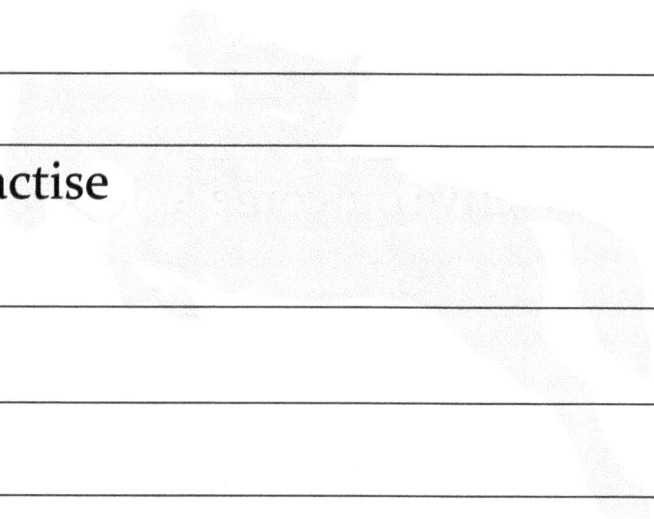

_____

_____

_____

Date _____   Time _____

Horse _____

Instructor _____

Discipline _____

The Lessons objectives

_____

_____

_____

Instructors comments

_____

_____

_____

Positive outcome of lesson

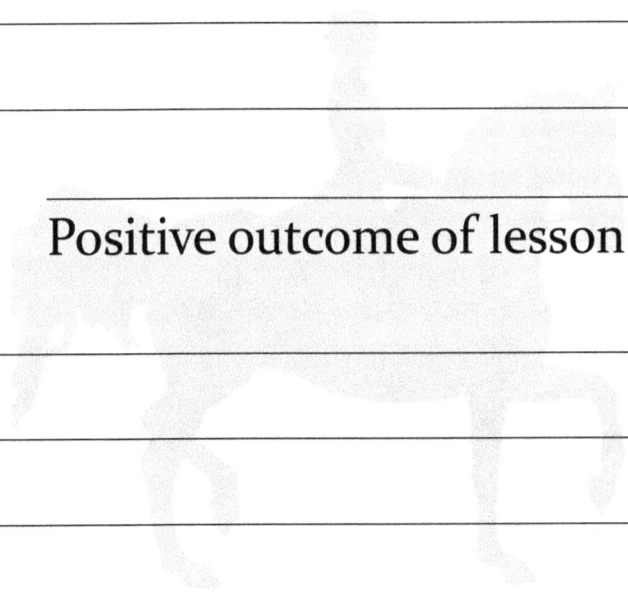

_____

_____

_____

About my performance

_____

_____

_____

About my Horses performance

_____

_____

_____

Transitions to practise

_____

_____

_____

Exercises to practise

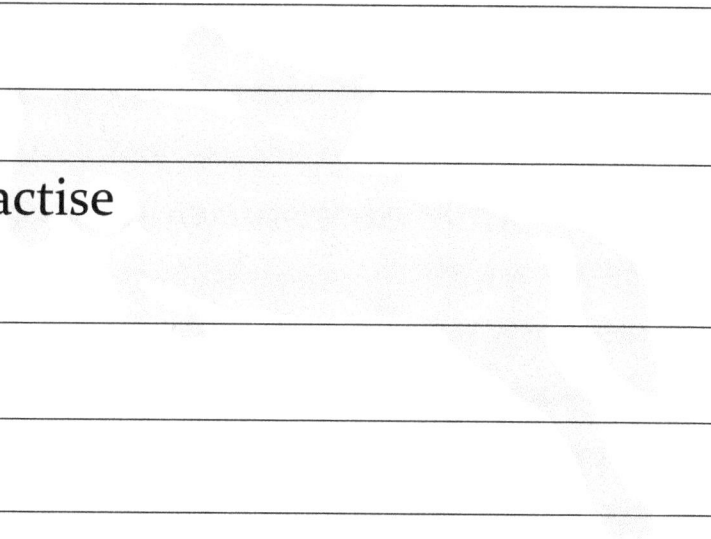

_____

_____

_____

Date _____ Time _____

Horse _____

Instructor _____

Discipline _____

The Lessons objectives

_____

_____

_____

Instructors comments

_____

_____

_____

Positive outcome of lesson

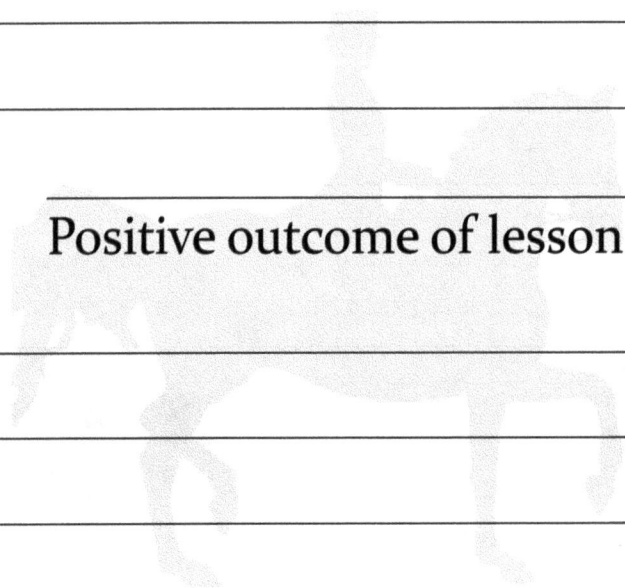

_____

_____

_____

About my performance

_____

_____

_____

_____

About my Horses performance

_____

_____

_____

_____

Transitions to practise

_____

_____

_____

_____

Exercises to practise

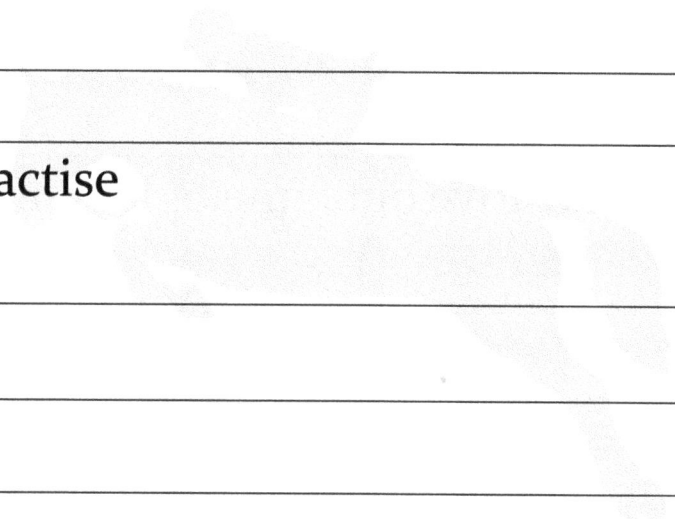

_____

_____

_____

_____

Date _____   Time _____

Horse _____

Instructor _____

Discipline _____

The Lessons objectives

_____

_____

_____

Instructors comments

_____

_____

_____

Positive outcome of lesson

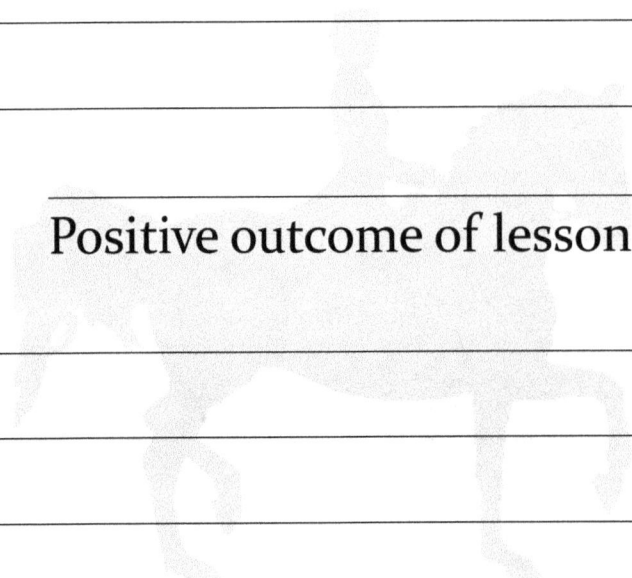

_____

_____

_____

About my performance

_____

_____

_____

About my Horses performance

_____

_____

_____

Transitions to practise

_____

_____

_____

Exercises to practise

_____

_____

_____

Date _____   Time _____

Horse   _____

Instructor   _____

Discipline   _____

The Lessons objectives

_____

_____

_____

Instructors comments

_____

_____

_____

Positive outcome of lesson

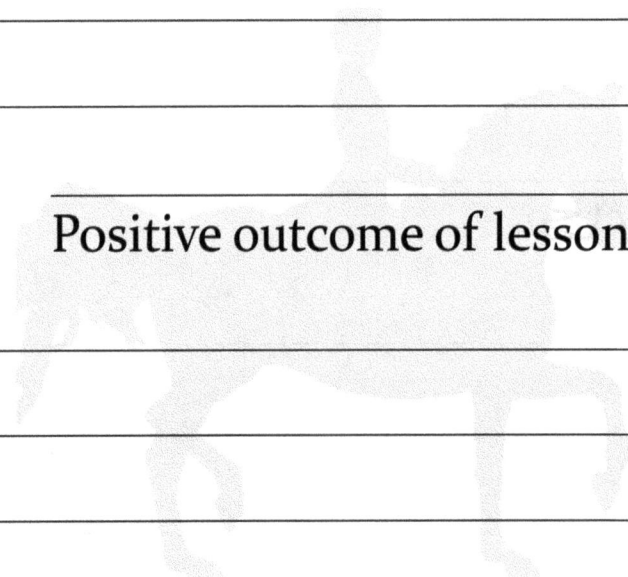

_____

_____

_____

About my performance

_____

_____

_____

About my Horses performance

_____

_____

_____

Transitions to practise

_____

_____

_____

Exercises to practise

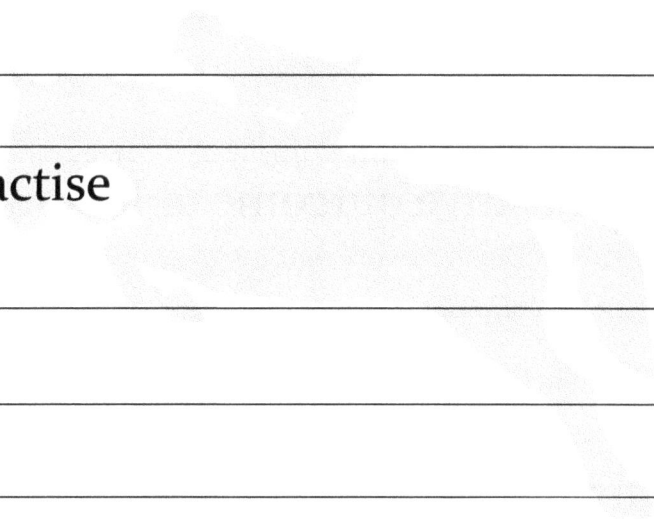

_____

_____

_____

Date _____   Time _____

Horse _____

Instructor _____

Discipline _____

The Lessons objectives

_____

_____

_____

Instructors comments

_____

_____

_____

Positive outcome of lesson

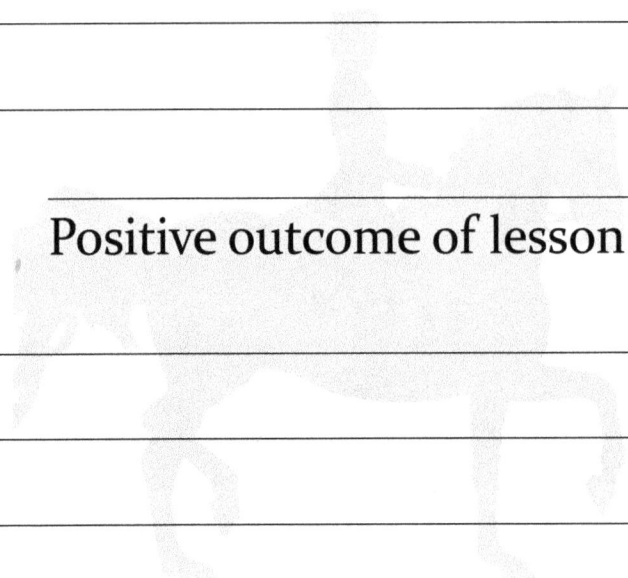

_____

_____

_____

About my performance

_____

_____

_____

_____

About my Horses performance

_____

_____

_____

_____

Transitions to practise

_____

_____

_____

_____

Exercises to practise

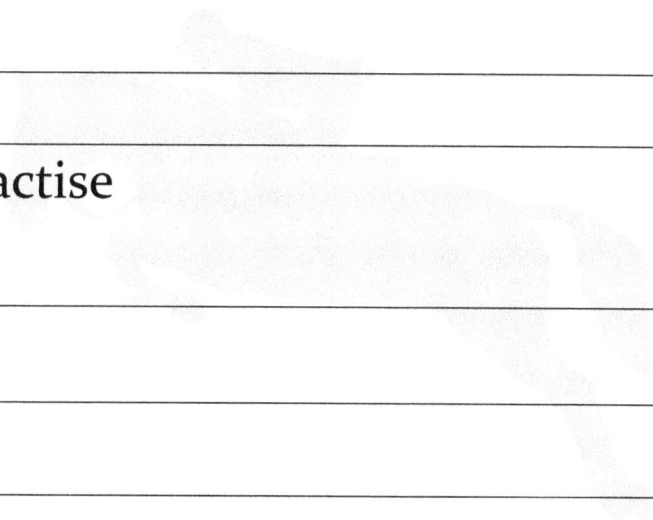

_____

_____

_____

Date _____   Time _____

Horse   _____

Instructor   _____

Discipline   _____

The Lessons objectives

_____

_____

_____

Instructors comments

_____

_____

_____

Positive outcome of lesson

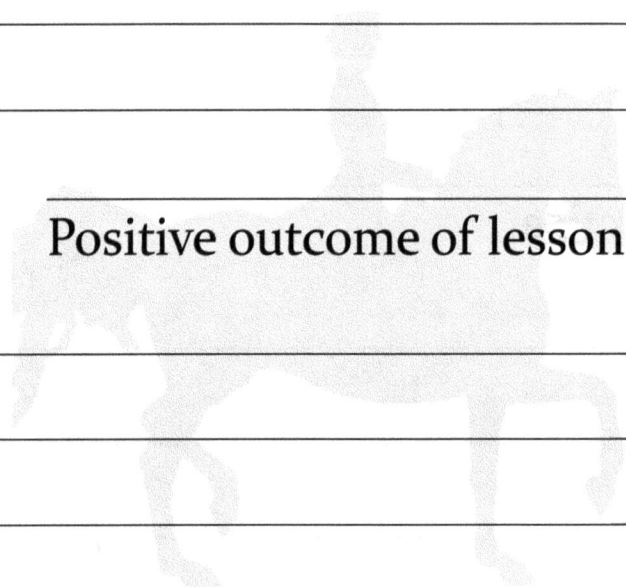

_____

_____

_____

About my performance

_____

_____

_____

_____

About my Horses performance

_____

_____

_____

_____

Transitions to practise

_____

_____

_____

_____

Exercises to practise

_____

_____

_____

_____

Date _____   Time _____

Horse _____

Instructor _____

Discipline _____

The Lessons objectives

_____

_____

_____

Instructors comments

_____

_____

_____

Positive outcome of lesson

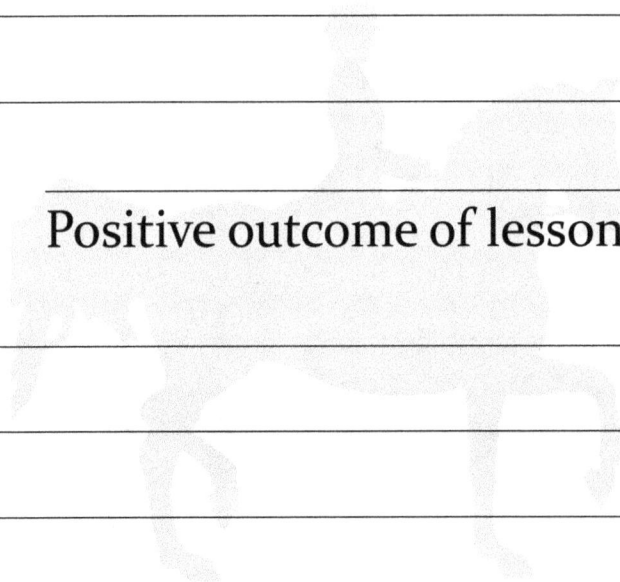

_____

_____

_____

About my performance

_____

_____

_____

About my Horses performance

_____

_____

_____

Transitions to practise

_____

_____

_____

Exercises to practise

_____

_____

_____

Date ———————— Time ——————

Horse ————————————————————————

Instructor ———————————————————————

Discipline ———————————————————————

The Lessons objectives

————————————————————————————

————————————————————————————

————————————————————————————

Instructors comments

————————————————————————————

————————————————————————————

————————————————————————————

Positive outcome of lesson

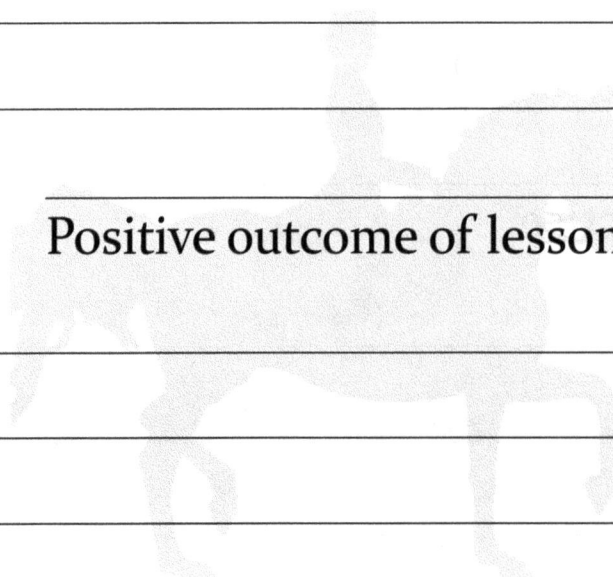

————————————————————————————

————————————————————————————

————————————————————————————

About my performance

_____

_____

_____

About my Horses performance

_____

_____

_____

Transitions to practise

_____

_____

_____

Exercises to practise

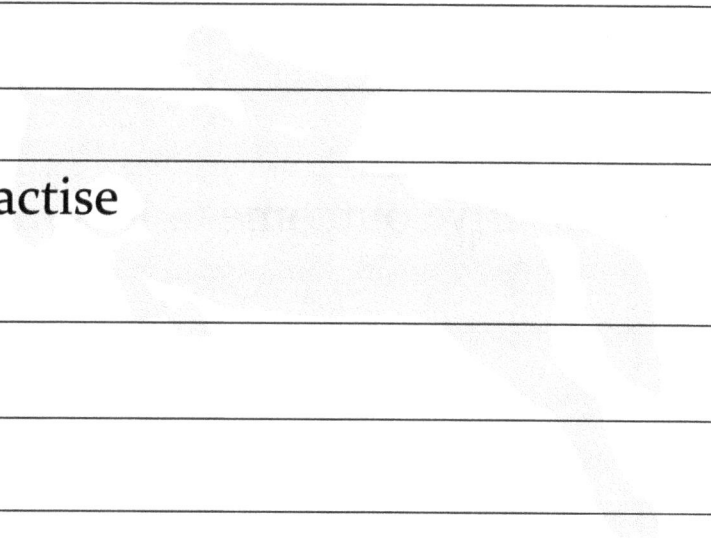

_____

_____

_____

Date _____   Time _____

Horse _____

Instructor _____

Discipline _____

The Lessons objectives

_____

_____

_____

Instructors comments

_____

_____

_____

Positive outcome of lesson

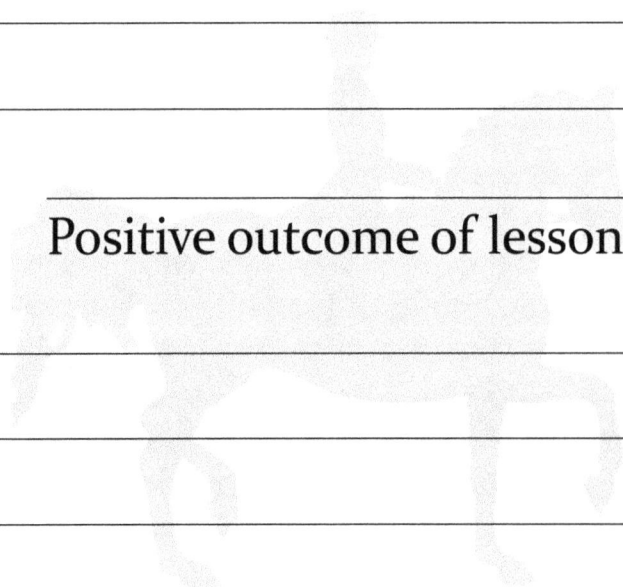

_____

_____

_____

About my performance

_____

_____

_____

About my Horses performance

_____

_____

_____

Transitions to practise

_____

_____

_____

Exercises to practise

_____

_____

_____

Date _____   Time _____

Horse _____

Instructor _____

Discipline _____

The Lessons objectives

_____

_____

_____

Instructors comments

_____

_____

_____

Positive outcome of lesson

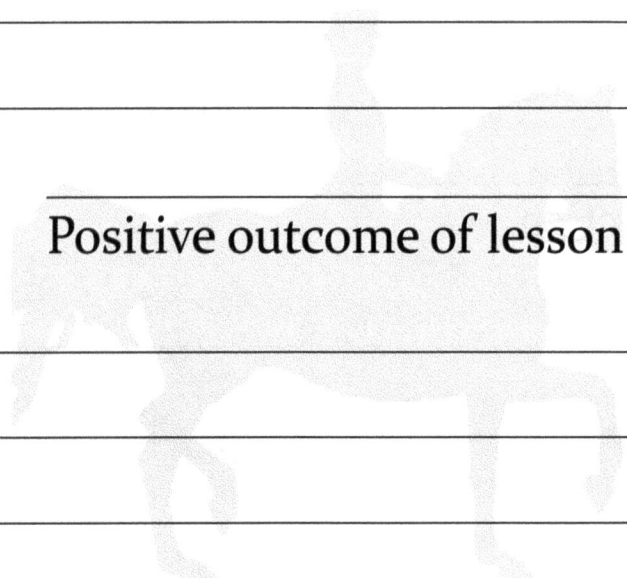

_____

_____

_____

About my performance

_____

_____

_____

About my Horses performance

_____

_____

_____

Transitions to practise

_____

_____

_____

Exercises to practise

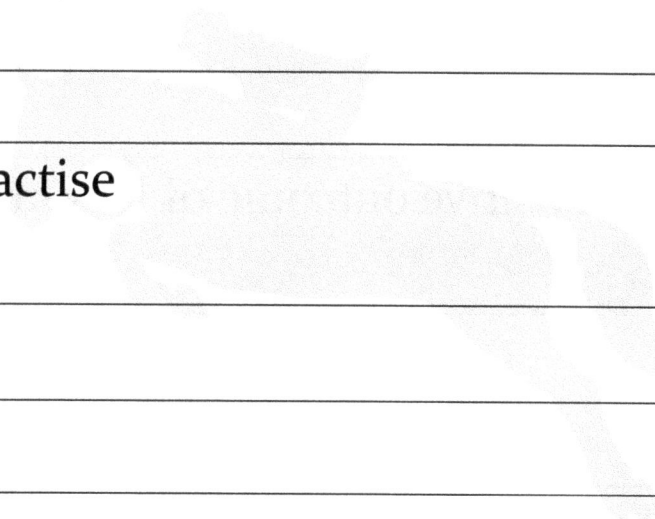

_____

_____

_____

Date _____   Time _____

Horse _____

Instructor _____

Discipline _____

The Lessons objectives

_____

_____

_____

Instructors comments

_____

_____

_____

Positive outcome of lesson

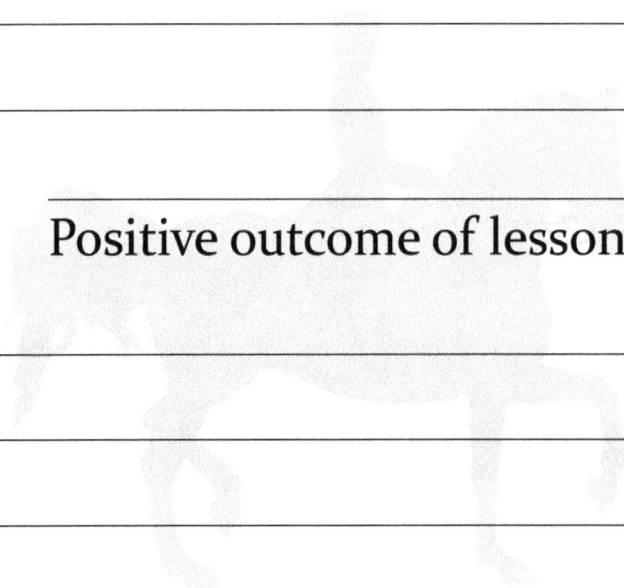

_____

_____

_____

About my performance

_____

_____

_____

About my Horses performance

_____

_____

_____

Transitions to practise

_____

_____

_____

Exercises to practise

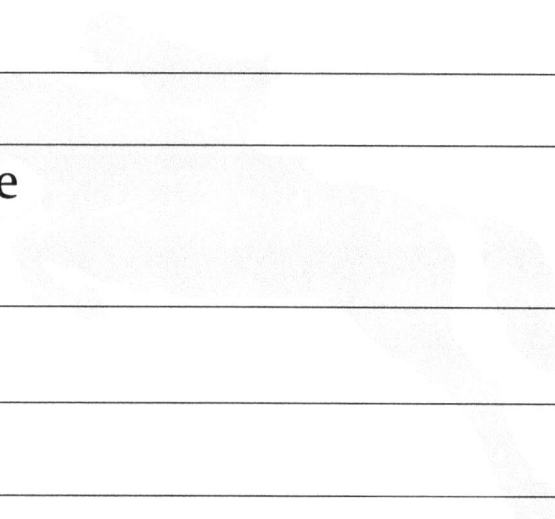

_____

_____

_____

Date _____   Time _____

Horse _____

Instructor _____

Discipline _____

The Lessons objectives

_____

_____

_____

Instructors comments

_____

_____

_____

Positive outcome of lesson

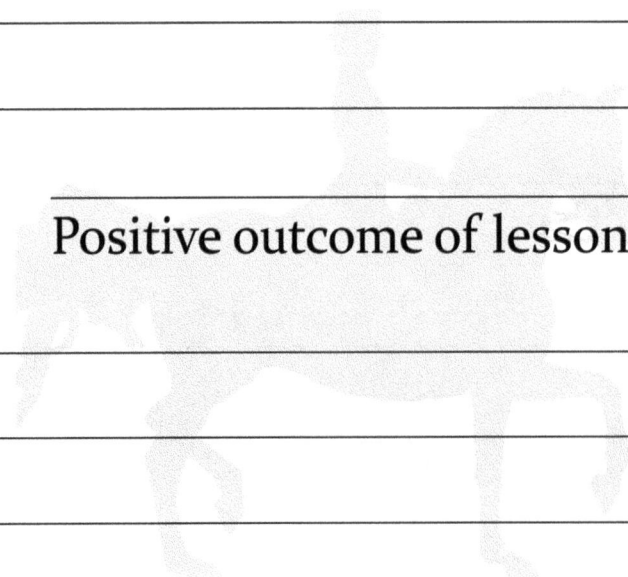

_____

_____

_____

About my performance

_____

_____

_____

About my Horses performance

_____

_____

_____

Transitions to practise

_____

_____

_____

Exercises to practise

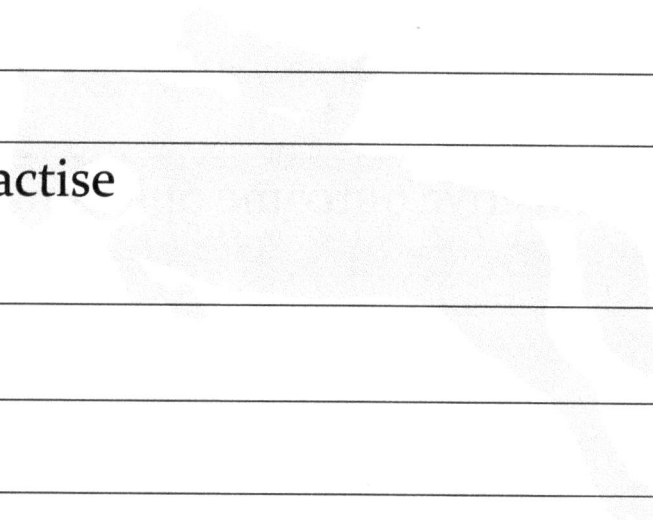

_____

_____

_____

Date ——————— Time ——————

Horse ——————————————————————

Instructor ——————————————————————

Discipline ——————————————————————

The Lessons objectives

——————————————————————————————

——————————————————————————————

——————————————————————————————

Instructors comments

——————————————————————————————

——————————————————————————————

——————————————————————————————

Positive outcome of lesson

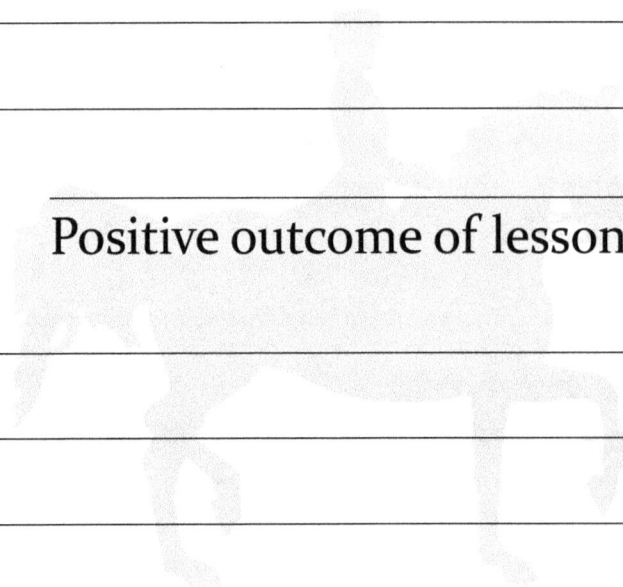

——————————————————————————————

——————————————————————————————

——————————————————————————————

About my performance

_____

_____

_____

About my Horses performance

_____

_____

_____

Transitions to practise

_____

_____

_____

Exercises to practise

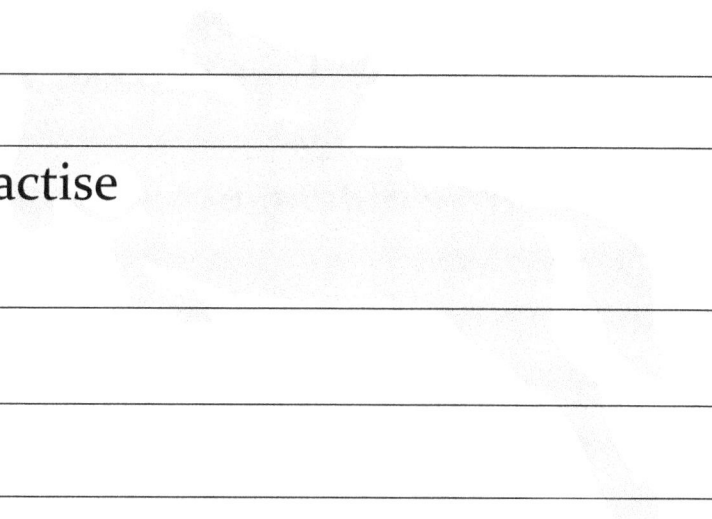

_____

_____

_____

Date _____ Time _____

Horse _____

Instructor _____

Discipline _____

The Lessons objectives

_____

_____

_____

Instructors comments

_____

_____

_____

Positive outcome of lesson

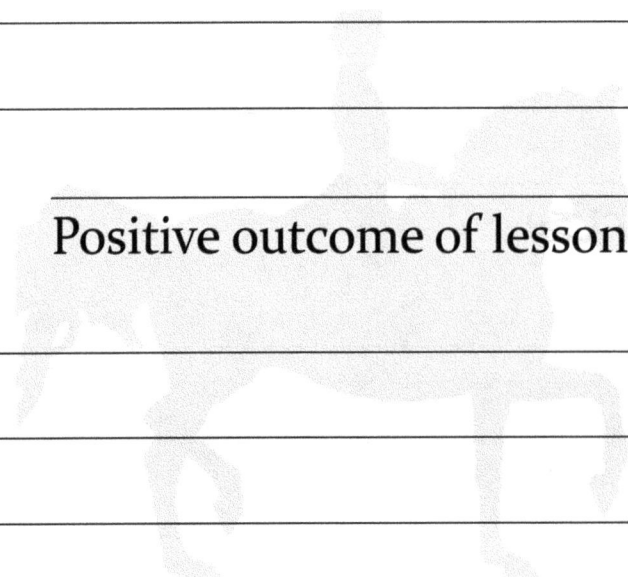

_____

_____

_____

About my performance

_____

_____

_____

About my Horses performance

_____

_____

_____

Transitions to practise

_____

_____

_____

Exercises to practise

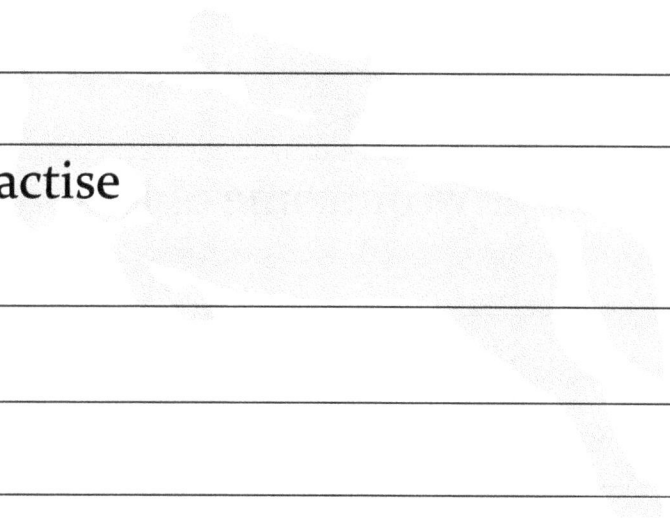

_____

_____

_____

Date ——————— Time ——————

Horse —————————————————————

Instructor —————————————————————

Discipline —————————————————————

The Lessons objectives

——————————————————————————————

——————————————————————————————

——————————————————————————————

Instructors comments

——————————————————————————————

——————————————————————————————

——————————————————————————————

Positive outcome of lesson

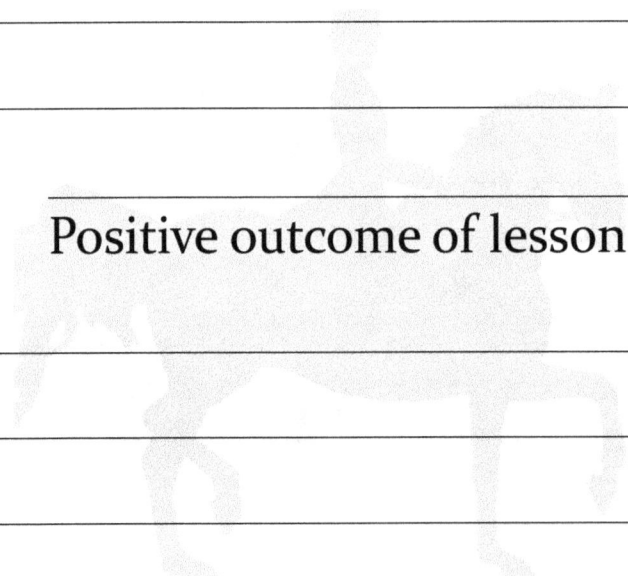

——————————————————————————————

——————————————————————————————

——————————————————————————————

About my performance

_____

_____

_____

About my Horses performance

_____

_____

_____

Transitions to practise

_____

_____

_____

Exercises to practise

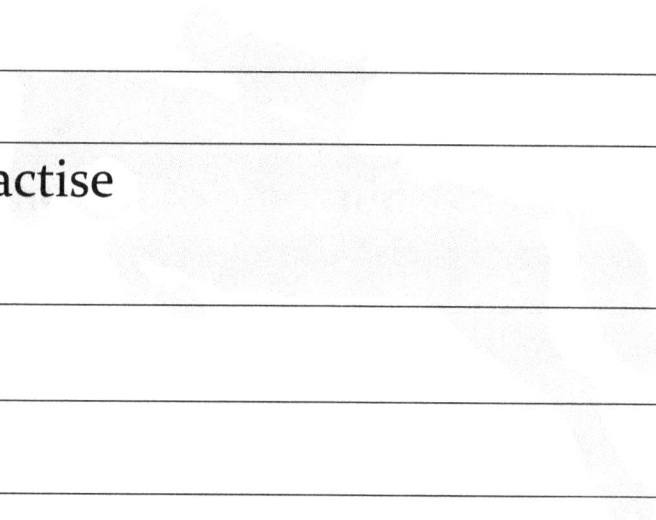

_____

_____

_____

Date _____ Time _____

Horse _____

Instructor _____

Discipline _____

The Lessons objectives

_____

_____

_____

Instructors comments

_____

_____

_____

Positive outcome of lesson

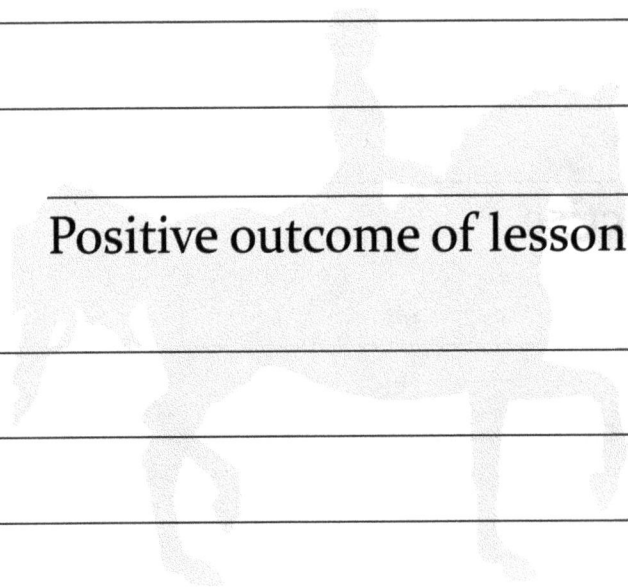

_____

_____

_____

About my performance

_____

_____

_____

About my Horses performance

_____

_____

_____

Transitions to practise

_____

_____

_____

Exercises to practise

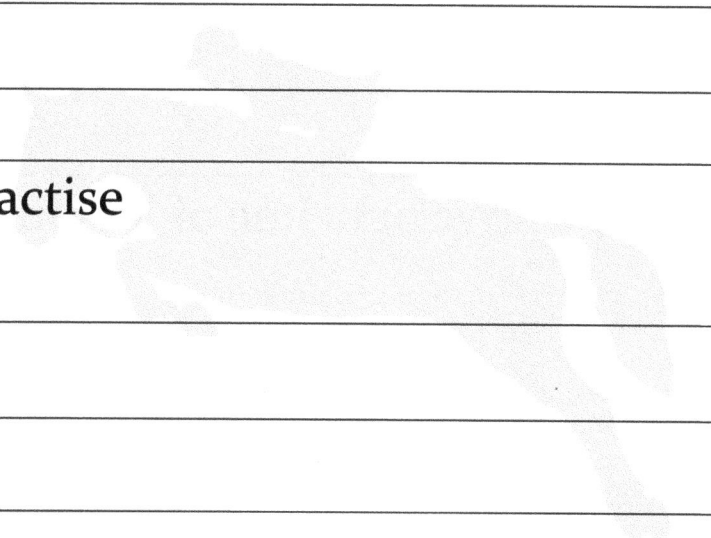

_____

_____

_____

Date _____   Time _____

Horse _____

Instructor _____

Discipline _____

The Lessons objectives

_____

_____

_____

Instructors comments

_____

_____

_____

Positive outcome of lesson

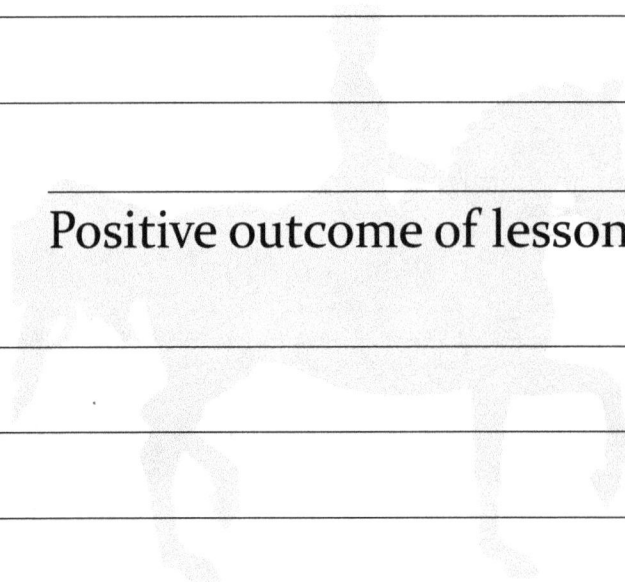

_____

_____

_____

About my performance

_____

_____

_____

About my Horses performance

_____

_____

_____

Transitions to practise

_____

_____

_____

Exercises to practise

_____

_____

_____

Date _____ Time _____

Horse _____

Instructor _____

Discipline _____

The Lessons objectives

_____

_____

_____

Instructors comments

_____

_____

_____

Positive outcome of lesson

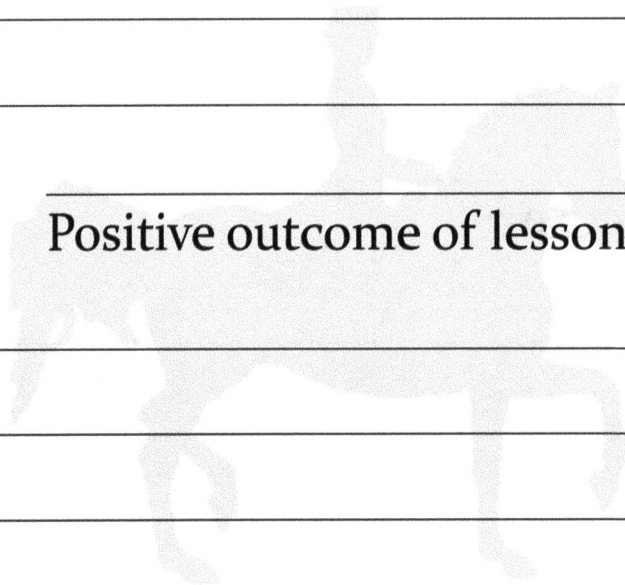

_____

_____

_____

About my performance

_____

_____

_____

_____

About my Horses performance

_____

_____

_____

Transitions to practise

_____

_____

_____

Exercises to practise

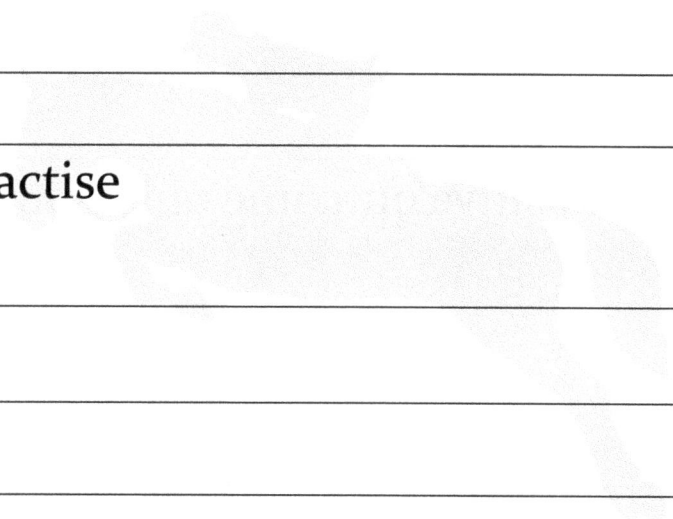

_____

_____

_____

Date _____   Time _____

Horse _____

Instructor _____

Discipline _____

The Lessons objectives

_____

_____

_____

Instructors comments

_____

_____

_____

Positive outcome of lesson

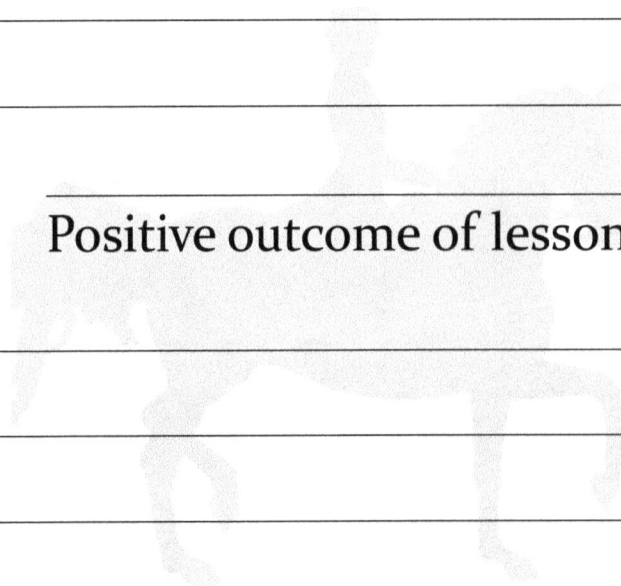

_____

_____

_____

About my performance

_____

_____

_____

About my Horses performance

_____

_____

_____

Transitions to practise

_____

_____

_____

Exercises to practise

_____

_____

_____

Date _____   Time _____

Horse _____

Instructor _____

Discipline _____

The Lessons objectives

_____

_____

_____

Instructors comments

_____

_____

_____

Positive outcome of lesson

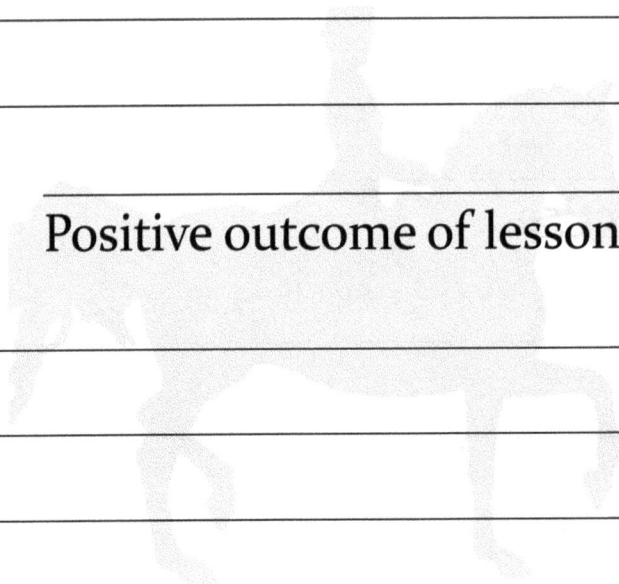

_____

_____

_____

About my performance

_____

_____

_____

_____

About my Horses performance

_____

_____

_____

Transitions to practise

_____

_____

_____

Exercises to practise

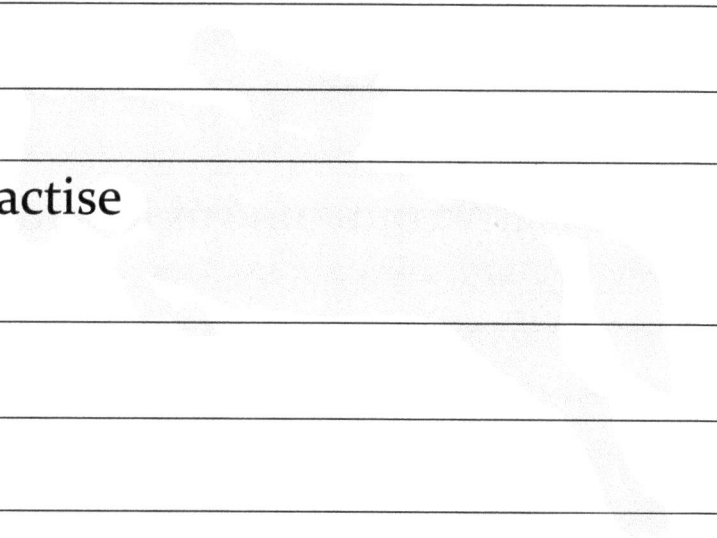

_____

_____

_____

Date _____   Time _____

Horse _____

Instructor _____

Discipline _____

The Lessons objectives

_____

_____

_____

Instructors comments

_____

_____

_____

Positive outcome of lesson

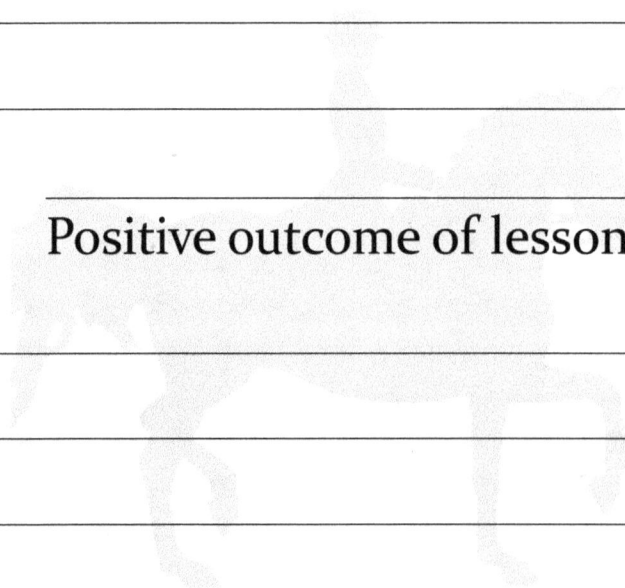

_____

_____

_____

About my performance

_____

_____

_____

About my Horses performance

_____

_____

_____

Transitions to practise

_____

_____

_____

Exercises to practise

_____

_____

_____

Date _____ Time _____

Horse _____

Instructor _____

Discipline _____

The Lessons objectives

_____

_____

_____

Instructors comments

_____

_____

_____

Positive outcome of lesson

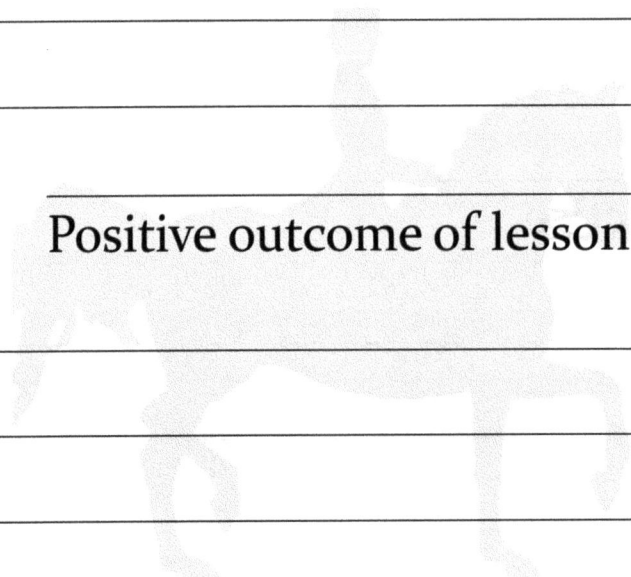

_____

_____

_____

About my performance

_____

_____

_____

About my Horses performance

_____

_____

_____

Transitions to practise

_____

_____

_____

Exercises to practise

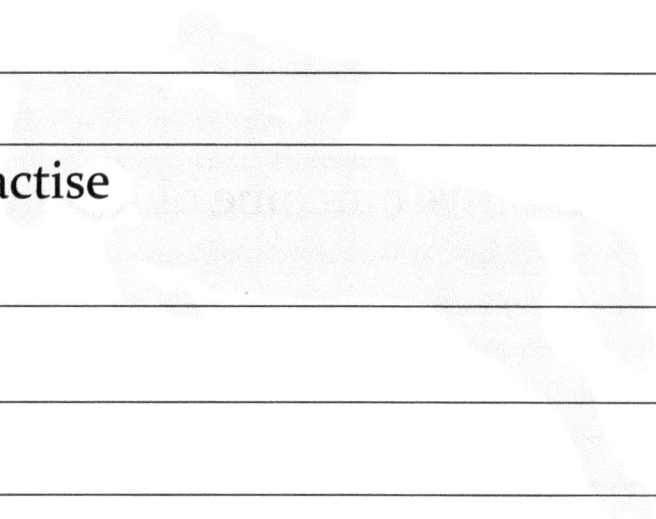

_____

_____

_____

Date ——————————— Time ——————————

Horse —————————————————————————————

Instructor —————————————————————————————

Discipline —————————————————————————————

The Lessons objectives

_____

_____

_____

Instructors comments

_____

_____

_____

Positive outcome of lesson

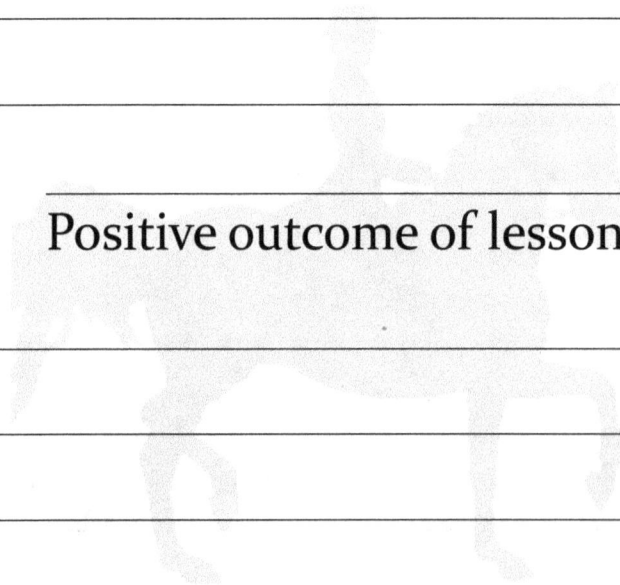

_____

_____

_____

About my performance

_____

_____

_____

About my Horses performance

_____

_____

_____

Transitions to practise

_____

_____

_____

Exercises to practise

_____

_____

_____

Date _____   Time _____

Horse _____

Instructor _____

Discipline _____

The Lessons objectives

_____

_____

_____

Instructors comments

_____

_____

_____

Positive outcome of lesson

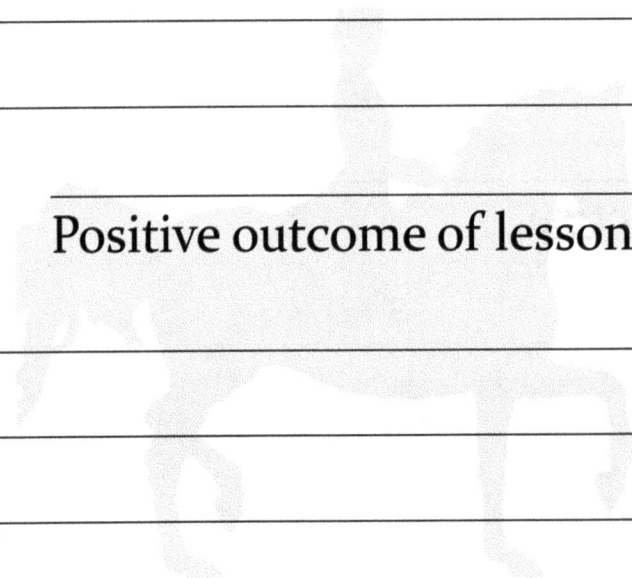

_____

_____

_____

About my performance

About my Horses performance

Transitions to practise

Exercises to practise

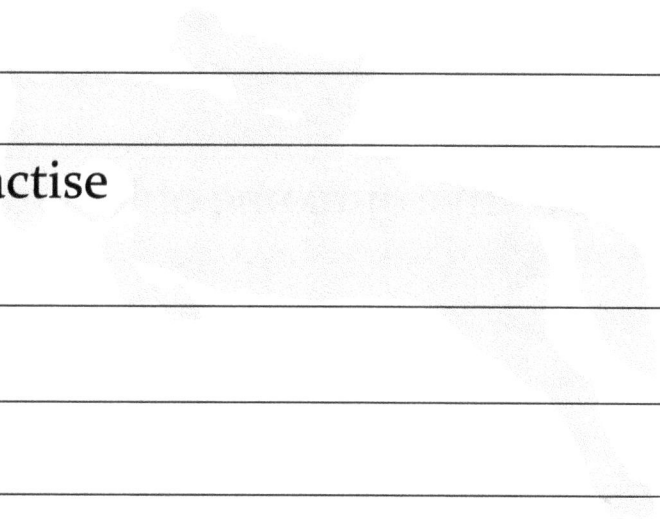

Date ——————— Time ————————

Horse ————————————————————————————

Instructor ————————————————————————

Discipline ————————————————————————

The Lessons objectives

————————————————————————————————

————————————————————————————————

————————————————————————————————

Instructors comments

————————————————————————————————

————————————————————————————————

————————————————————————————————

Positive outcome of lesson

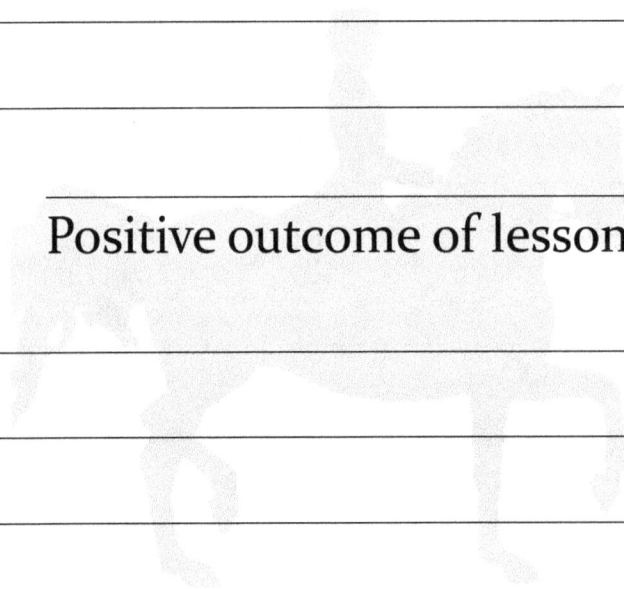

————————————————————————————————

————————————————————————————————

————————————————————————————————

About my performance

_____

_____

_____

About my Horses performance

_____

_____

_____

Transitions to practise

_____

_____

_____

Exercises to practise

_____

_____

_____

Date _____   Time _____

Horse _____

Instructor _____

Discipline _____

The Lessons objectives

_____

_____

_____

Instructors comments

_____

_____

_____

Positive outcome of lesson

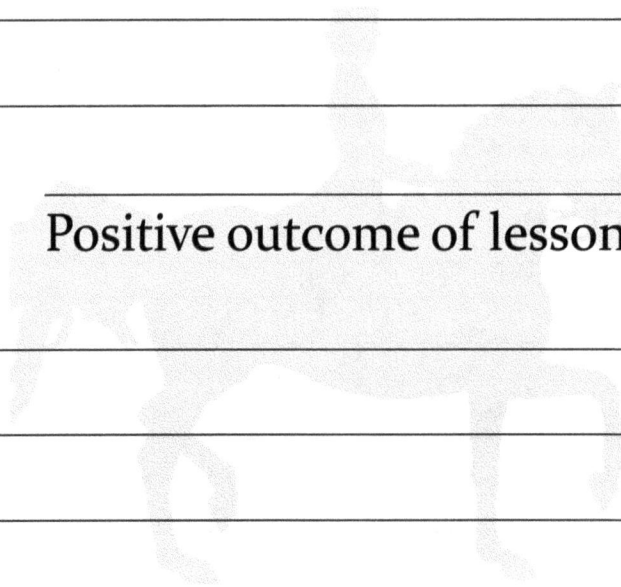

_____

_____

_____

About my performance

_____

_____

_____

_____

About my Horses performance

_____

_____

_____

_____

Transitions to practise

_____

_____

_____

_____

Exercises to practise

_____

_____

_____

Date _____   Time _____

Horse _____

Instructor _____

Discipline _____

The Lessons objectives

_____

_____

_____

Instructors comments

_____

_____

_____

Positive outcome of lesson

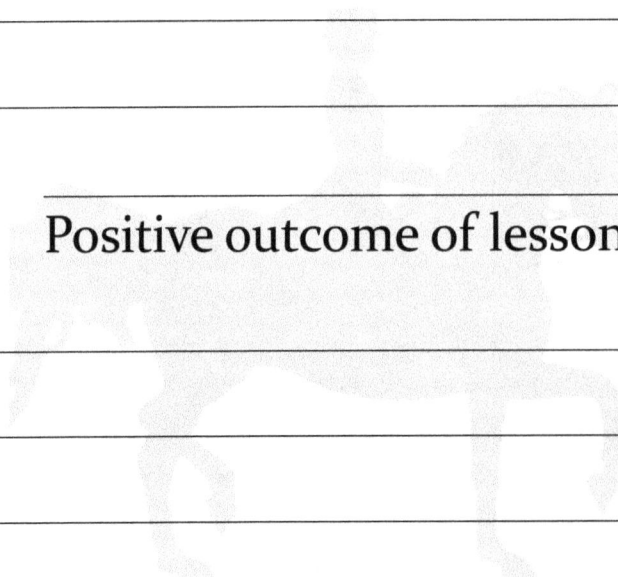

_____

_____

_____

About my performance

_____

_____

_____

About my Horses performance

_____

_____

_____

Transitions to practise

_____

_____

_____

Exercises to practise

_____

_____

_____

Date _____   Time _____

Horse _____

Instructor _____

Discipline _____

The Lessons objectives

_____

_____

_____

Instructors comments

_____

_____

_____

Positive outcome of lesson

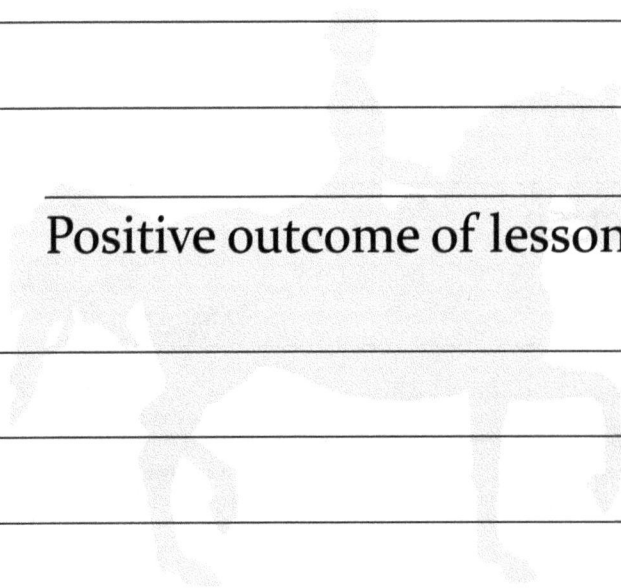

_____

_____

_____

About my performance

_____

_____

_____

About my Horses performance

_____

_____

_____

Transitions to practise

_____

_____

_____

Exercises to practise

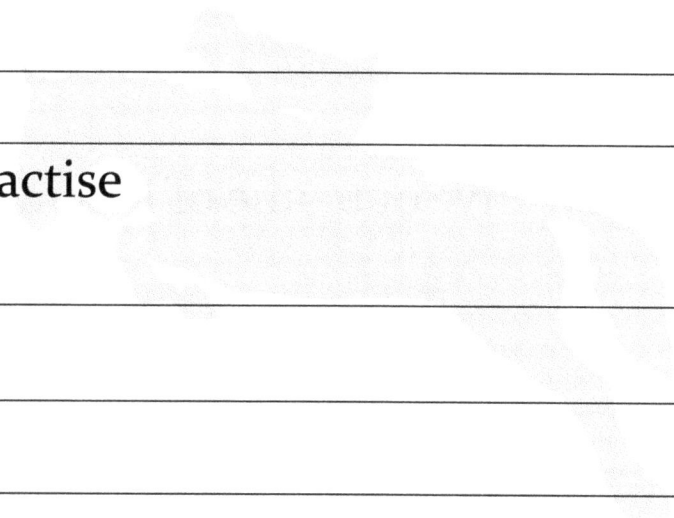

_____

_____

_____

Date ——————   Time ——————

Horse ———————————————————————

Instructor ———————————————————————

Discipline ———————————————————————

The Lessons objectives

———————————————————————

———————————————————————

———————————————————————

Instructors comments

———————————————————————

———————————————————————

———————————————————————

Positive outcome of lesson

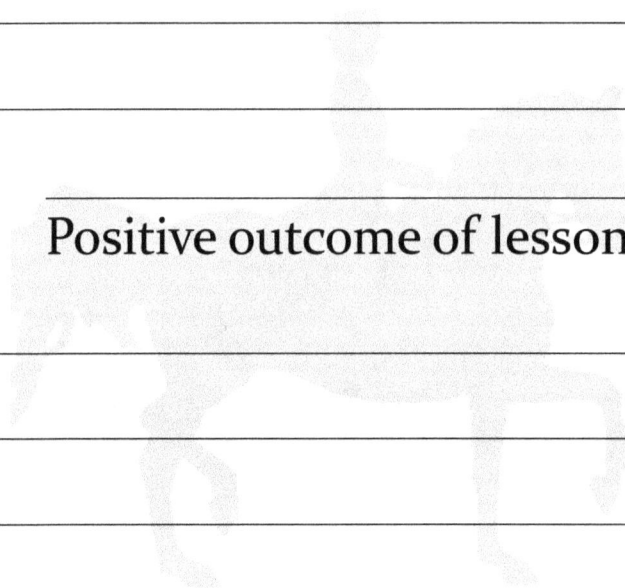

———————————————————————

———————————————————————

———————————————————————

About my performance

_____

_____

_____

_____

About my Horses performance

_____

_____

_____

_____

Transitions to practise

_____

_____

_____

_____

Exercises to practise

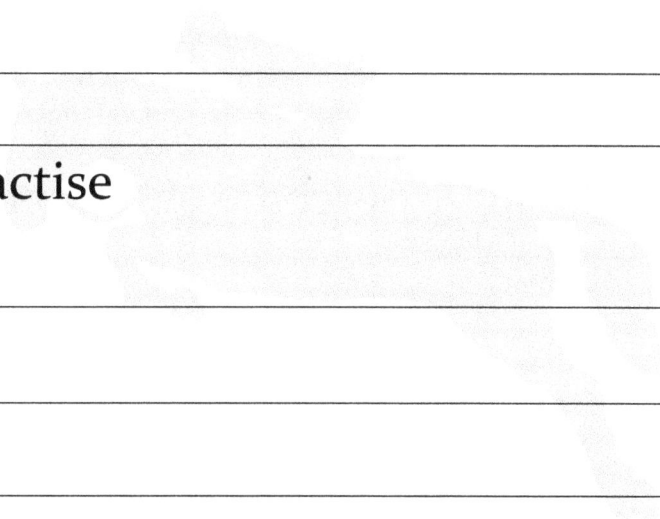

_____

_____

_____

Date _____ Time _____

Horse _____

Instructor _____

Discipline _____

The Lessons objectives

_____

_____

_____

Instructors comments

_____

_____

_____

Positive outcome of lesson

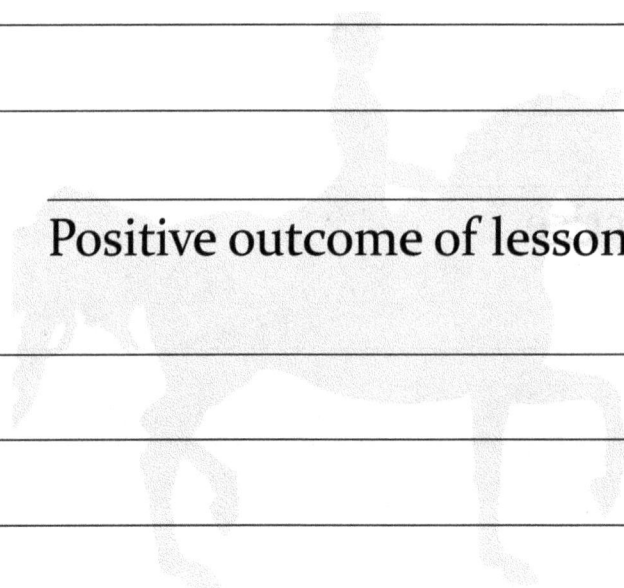

_____

_____

_____

About my performance

_____

_____

_____

_____

About my Horses performance

_____

_____

_____

_____

Transitions to practise

_____

_____

_____

Exercises to practise

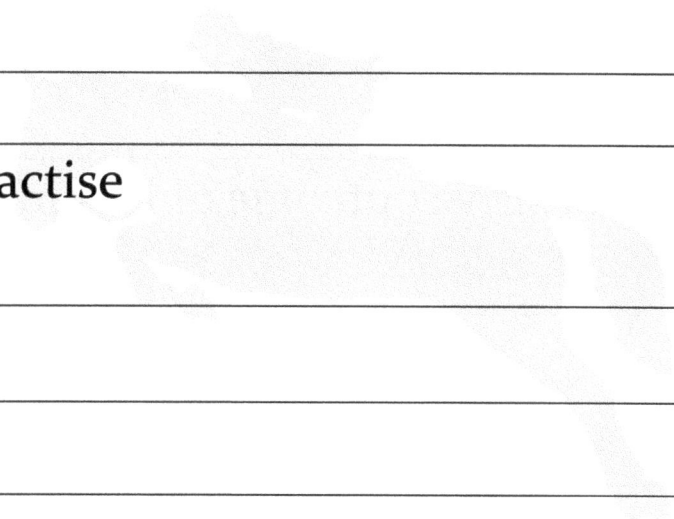

_____

_____

_____

Date _____ Time _____

Horse _____

Instructor _____

Discipline _____

The Lessons objectives

_____

_____

_____

Instructors comments

_____

_____

_____

Positive outcome of lesson

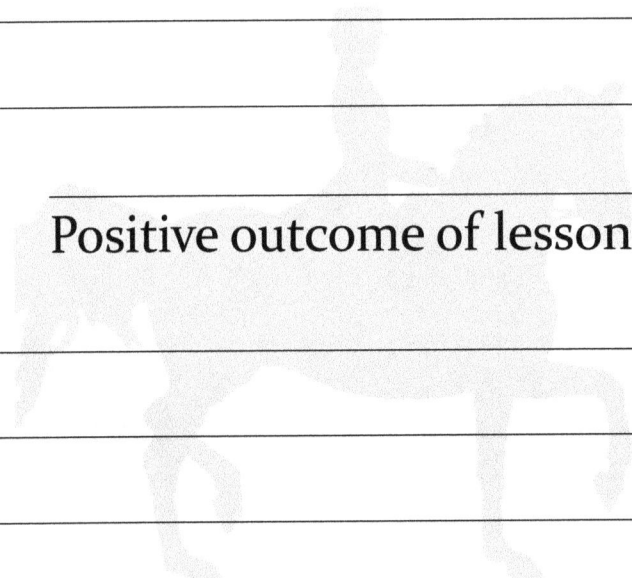

_____

_____

_____

About my performance

_____

_____

_____

About my Horses performance

_____

_____

_____

Transitions to practise

_____

_____

_____

Exercises to practise

_____

_____

_____

Date ——————————— Time ———————

Horse ———————————————————————————

Instructor ——————————————————————

Discipline ——————————————————————

The Lessons objectives

———————————————————————————————

———————————————————————————————

———————————————————————————————

Instructors comments

———————————————————————————————

———————————————————————————————

———————————————————————————————

Positive outcome of lesson

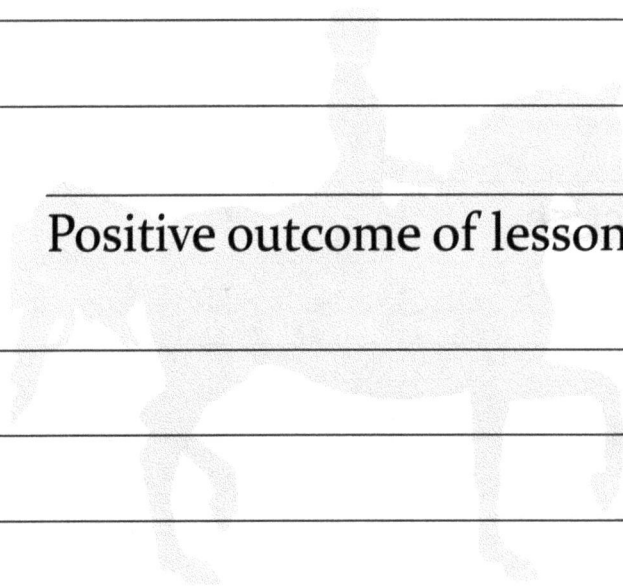

———————————————————————————————

———————————————————————————————

———————————————————————————————

About my performance

_____

_____

_____

About my Horses performance

_____

_____

_____

Transitions to practise

_____

_____

_____

Exercises to practise

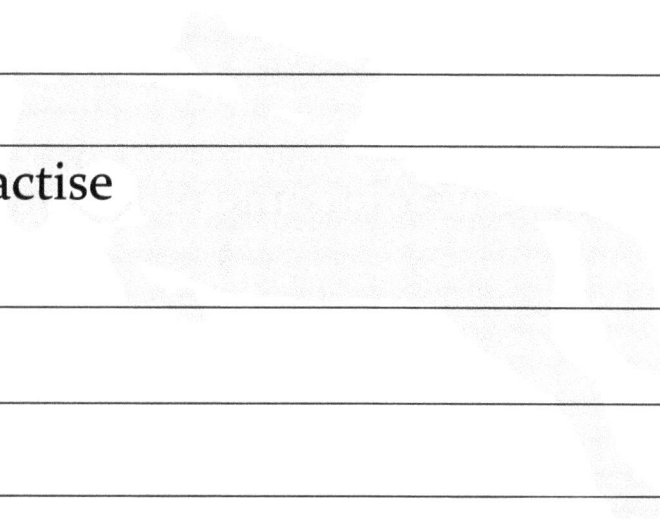

_____

_____

_____

Date _____   Time _____

Horse _____

Instructor _____

Discipline _____

The Lessons objectives

_____

_____

_____

Instructors comments

_____

_____

_____

Positive outcome of lesson

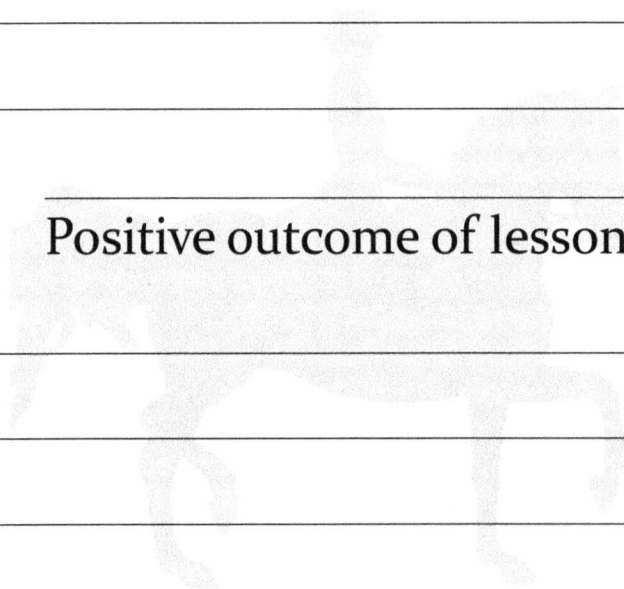

_____

_____

_____

About my performance

_____

_____

_____

About my Horses performance

_____

_____

_____

Transitions to practise

_____

_____

_____

Exercises to practise

_____

_____

_____

Date _____   Time _____

Horse _____

Instructor _____

Discipline _____

The Lessons objectives

_____

_____

_____

Instructors comments

_____

_____

_____

Positive outcome of lesson

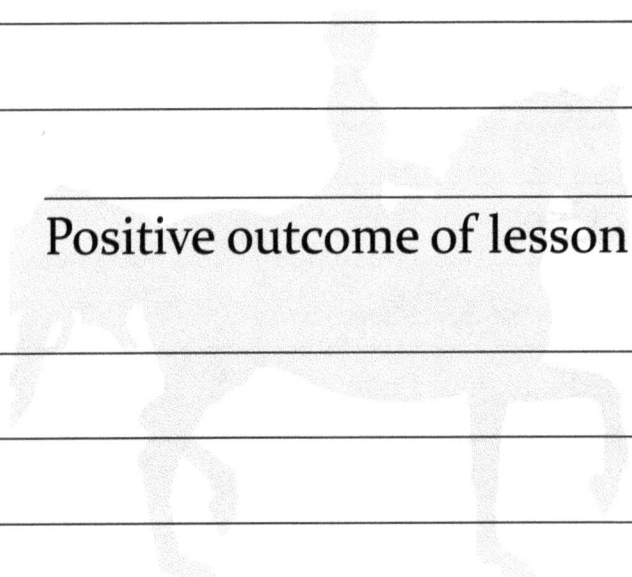

_____

_____

_____

About my performance

_____

_____

_____

_____

About my Horses performance

_____

_____

_____

_____

Transitions to practise

_____

_____

_____

Exercises to practise

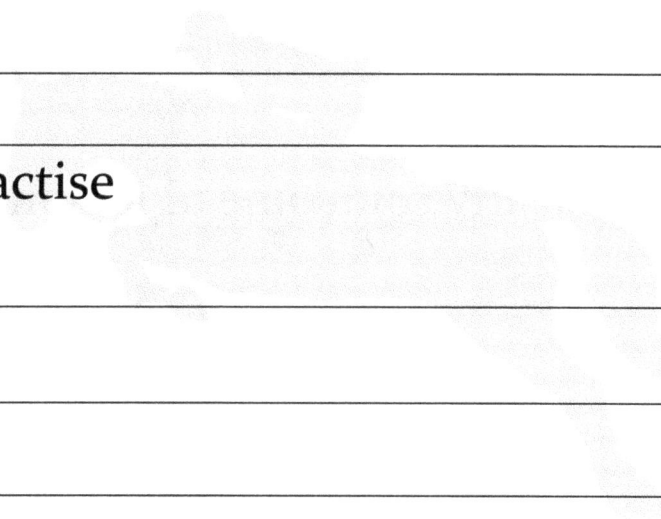

_____

_____

_____

Date _____ Time _____

Horse _____

Instructor _____

Discipline _____

The Lessons objectives

_____

_____

_____

Instructors comments

_____

_____

_____

Positive outcome of lesson

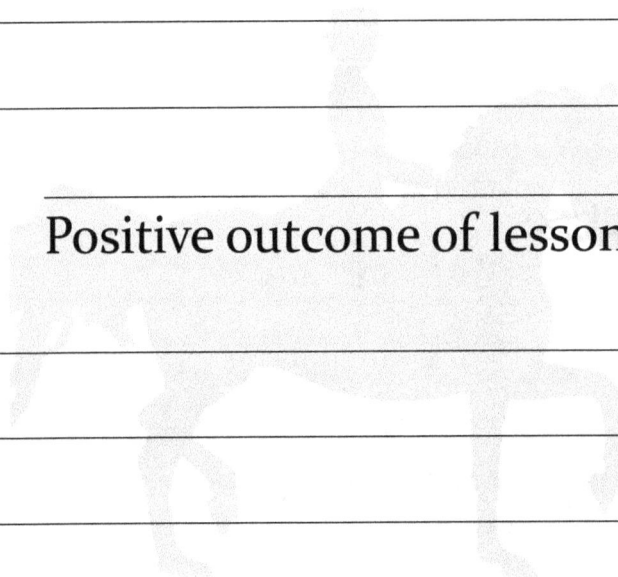

_____

_____

_____

About my performance

_____

_____

_____

_____

About my Horses performance

_____

_____

_____

_____

Transitions to practise

_____

_____

_____

_____

Exercises to practise

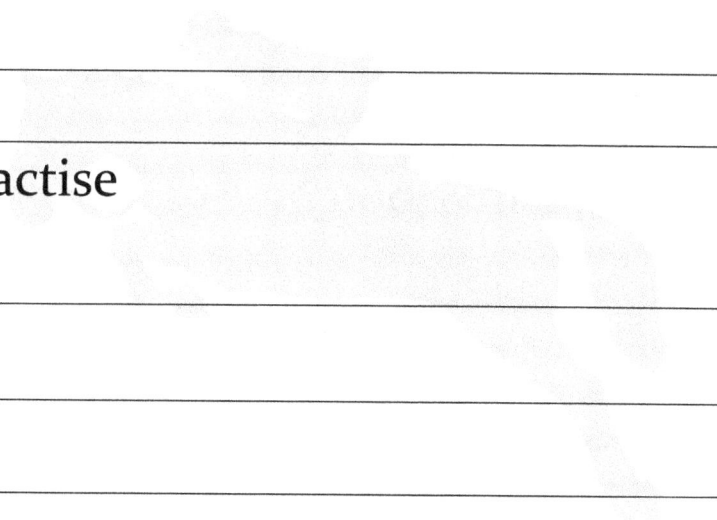

_____

_____

_____

Date _____ Time _____

Horse _____

Instructor _____

Discipline _____

The Lessons objectives

_____

_____

_____

Instructors comments

_____

_____

_____

_____

Positive outcome of lesson

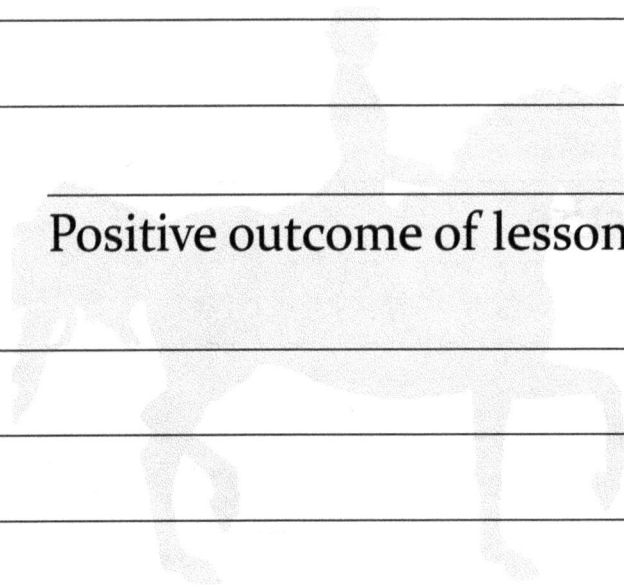

_____

_____

_____

About my performance

About my Horses performance

Transitions to practise

Exercises to practise

Date _____   Time _____

Horse _____

Instructor _____

Discipline _____

The Lessons objectives

_____

_____

_____

Instructors comments

_____

_____

_____

Positive outcome of lesson

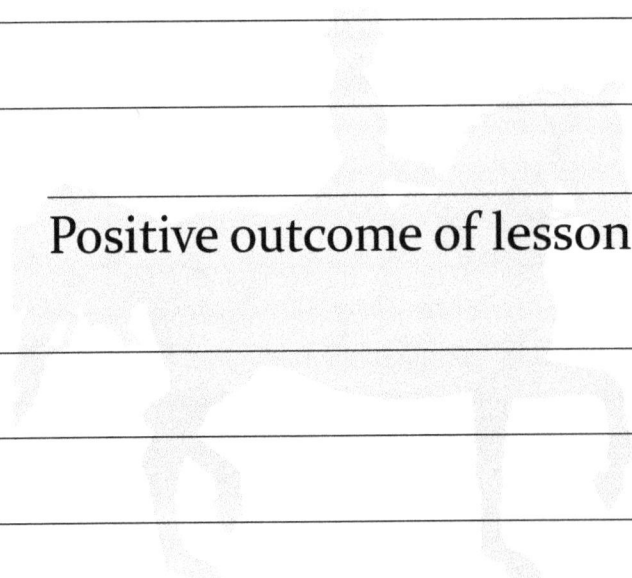

_____

_____

_____

About my performance

_____

_____

_____

About my Horses performance

_____

_____

_____

Transitions to practise

_____

_____

_____

Exercises to practise

_____

_____

_____

Date _____   Time _____

Horse _____

Instructor _____

Discipline _____

The Lessons objectives

_____

_____

_____

Instructors comments

_____

_____

_____

Positive outcome of lesson

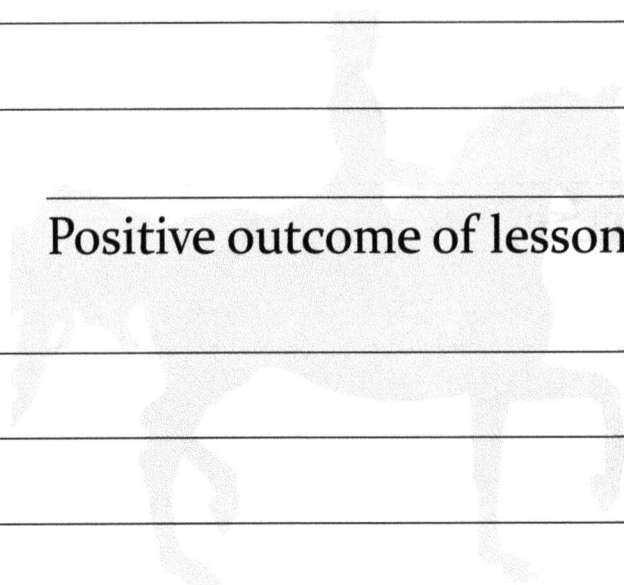

_____

_____

_____

About my performance

_____

_____

_____

About my Horses performance

_____

_____

_____

Transitions to practise

_____

_____

_____

Exercises to practise

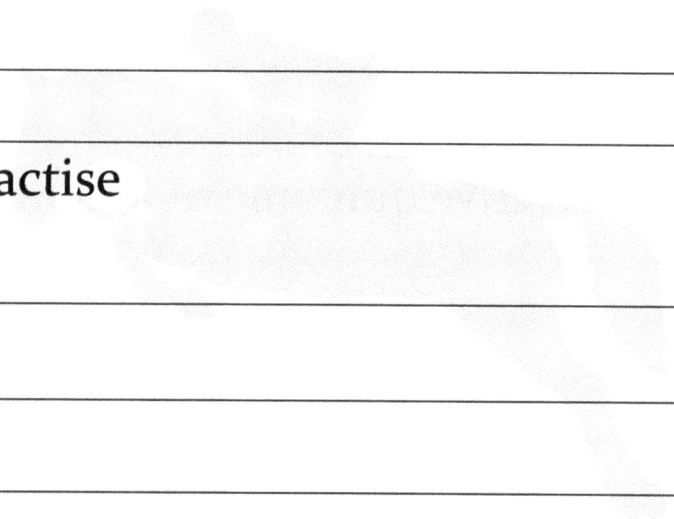

_____

_____

_____

Date _____ Time _____

Horse _____

Instructor _____

Discipline _____

The Lessons objectives

_____

_____

_____

Instructors comments

_____

_____

_____

Positive outcome of lesson

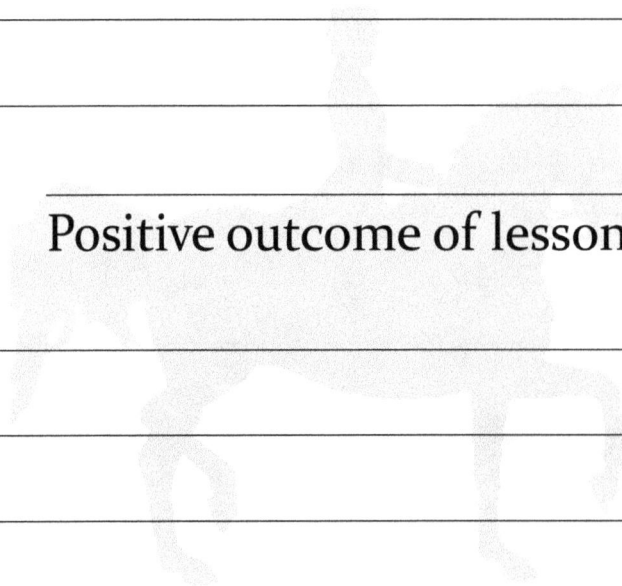

_____

_____

_____

About my performance

_____

_____

_____

About my Horses performance

_____

_____

_____

Transitions to practise

_____

_____

_____

Exercises to practise

_____

_____

_____

Date _____   Time _____

Horse   _____

Instructor   _____

Discipline   _____

The Lessons objectives

_____

_____

_____

Instructors comments

_____

_____

_____

_____

Positive outcome of lesson

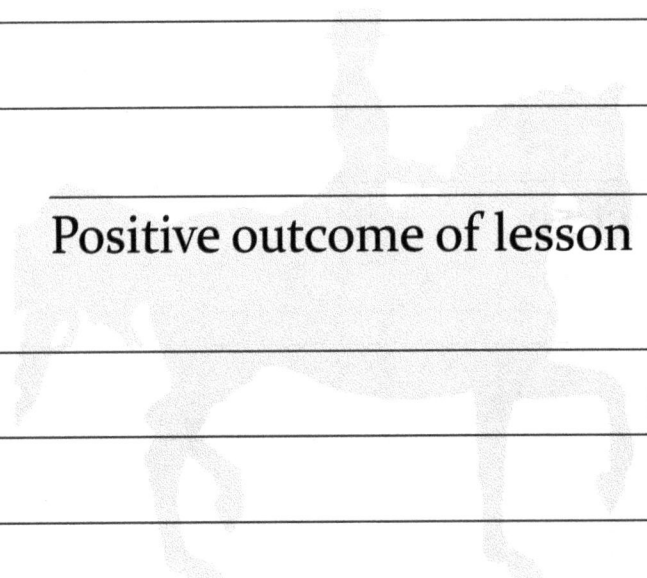

_____

_____

_____

About my performance

_____

_____

_____

_____

About my Horses performance

_____

_____

_____

Transitions to practise

_____

_____

_____

Exercises to practise

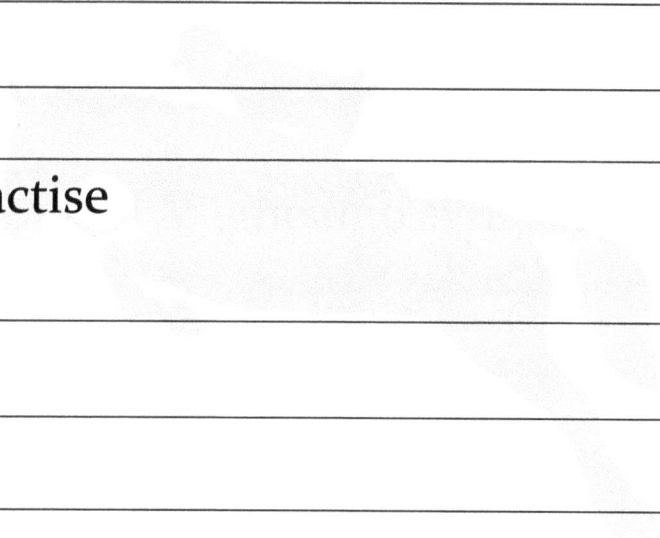

_____

_____

_____

Date _____   Time _____

Horse _____

Instructor _____

Discipline _____

The Lessons objectives

_____

_____

_____

Instructors comments

_____

_____

_____

Positive outcome of lesson

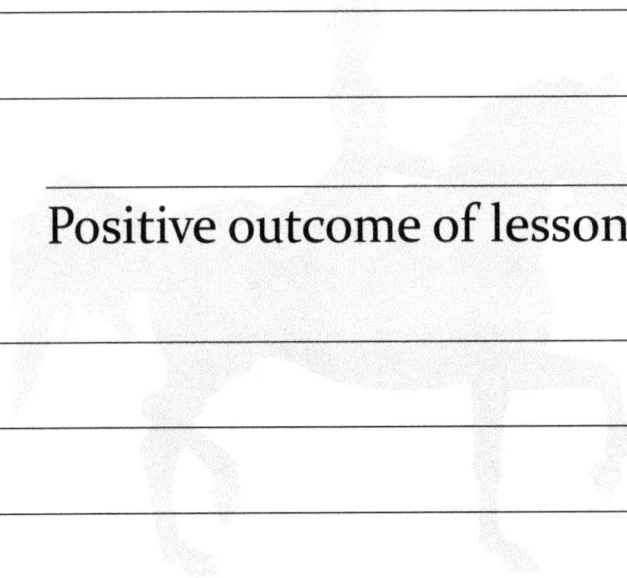

_____

_____

_____

About my performance

_____

_____

_____

_____

About my Horses performance

_____

_____

_____

_____

Transitions to practise

_____

_____

_____

_____

Exercises to practise

_____

_____

_____